G000151261

LAW OF FIELD SPORTS

LAW OF FIELD SPORTS

Tim Russ and Jamie Foster

WS
&H

Wildy, Simmonds & Hill Publishing

Copyright © 2010 Tim Russ and Jamie Foster

Crown copyright material is reproduced under the terms of the Click-Use Licence

Law of Field Sports

British Library Cataloguing in Publication Data
A catalogue record for this book is available from the British Library

ISBN 9780854900695

Typeset in Baskerville MT Pro and Optima LT by Cornubia Press Ltd
Printed and bound in the United Kingdom by Antony Rowe Ltd, Chippenham, Wiltshire

The right of Tim Russ and Jamie Foster to be identified as the authors of this Work has been asserted by them in accordance with sections 77 and 78 of the Copyright, Designs and Patents Act 1988

All rights reserved. No part of this book may be reproduced, stored in a retrieval system, or transmitted, in any form or by any means, electronic, mechanical, photocopying, recording or otherwise, without the consent of the copyright owners, application for which should be addressed to the publisher. Such a written permission must also be obtained before any part of this publication is stored in a retrieval system of any nature.

First published in 2010 by
Wildy, Simmonds & Hill Publishing
58 Carey Street
London WC2A 2JF
England

Contents

Table of Cases

References are to page numbers

Table of Statutes

Table of Statutory Instruments

References are to page numbers

Table of International Material

Foreword

Law books rarely hold any appeal for the layperson. Written for lawyers as tools of the trade, they are usually hard to follow and almost never entertaining.

This book is a rare exception.

Not only is this a much needed comprehensive and comprehensible guide to the maze of laws relating to game and countryside pursuits for both legal practitioners and non-lawyers alike, but also an entertaining history of game laws and cases to the present day.

What is game? When can you hunt legally? What, if anything, are you allowed to do with a badger? Does the law give you protection from a neighbour's pheasants which destroy your crops? Is it legal to shoot a dog chasing a hare on your land?

The answers to all these questions, and many more, are provided here by Jamie Foster, a lawyer who has been at the forefront of recent leading cases brought under the Hunting Act 2004. There is also an invaluable contribution from Tim Russ that will provide a full account of the civil law as it affects field sports.

No one who hunts, shoots, farms or indeed anyone who has an interest in the countryside and its wildlife should be without a copy.

What is more, unlike any other law book I have encountered, it is fun to read!

Baroness Ann Mallalieu
President of the Countryside Alliance

Introduction

There is much in common between the Game Act 1831 and the Hunting Act 2004. Both are in need of urgent reform but for different reasons. The former has become archaic and has been overtaken by changes in society's mores and habits. The latter, despite the vast amount of parliamentary time spent on it, was badly drafted, and through interpretation by case law, has become unworkable. These are not the only statutes affecting country sports there are of course others and an examination of them in all areas of the law of field sports, whether in respect of ground game or poaching leads to similar conclusions; there is an urgent need for reform.

Such reform was partially embraced by the Government in 2007 with the passing of the Regulatory Reform (Game) Order[1] (RRO) in that year. However, the restrictions on what an RRO can achieve lead to incomplete and unsatisfactory reform; an end to game licensing but nothing else touched.

There has been no textbook aimed at lawyers touching on the subjects covered by this book for the best part of a century. The aim of the book is to consider the statutes and relevant case law and then to provide analysis for amongst other things those drafting game rights in sporting or farming leases or defending those who might fall foul of the law and be facing prosecution in relation to game issues.

A consideration of the statutes which regulate the law of field sports may involve some repletion as there are relatively few of them. Where needed to secure brevity the following abbreviations have been used in the text of this book:

---

[1]   SI 2007/2007.

Statute	Abbreviation
Agricultural Holdings Act 1986	AHA 1986
Agricultural Tenancies Act 1995	ATA 1995
Animal Welfare Act 2006	AWA 2006
Deer Act 1991	DA 1991
Game Act 1831	GA 1831
Game Laws (Amendment) Act 1960	GLAA 1960
Ground Game Act 1880	GGA 1880
Hunting Act 2004	HA 2004
Law of Property Act 1925	LPA 1925
Night Poaching Act 1828	NPA 1828
Night Poaching Act 1840	NPA 1840
Poaching Prevention Act 1862	PPA 1862
Protection of Badgers Act 1992	PBA 1992
Regulatory Reform (Game) Order 2007	RRO 2007
Wildlife and Countryside Act 1981	WCA 1981

The offences referred to in this book are nearly all punishable after conviction at a summary trial with a fine on the standard scale. To save looking up the fines, Criminal Justice Act 1982, s 37 is set out below together with the table it creates:

The standard scale of fines for summary offences

(1) There shall be a standard scale of fines for summary offences, which shall be known as 'the standard scale'.

(2) The standard scale is shown below—

Level on the scale	Amount of fine
1	£200
2	£500
3	£1,000
4	£2,500
5	£5,000

(3) Where any enactment (whether contained in an Act passed before or after this Act) provides—

(a) that a person convicted of a summary offence shall be liable on conviction to a fine or a maximum fine by reference to a specified level on the standard scale; or

(b) confers power by subordinate instrument to make a person liable on conviction of a summary offence (whether or not created by the instrument) to a fine or maximum fine by reference to a specified level on the standard scale,

it is to be construed as referring to the standard scale for which this section provides as that standard scale has effect from time to time by virtue either of this section or of an order under section 143 of the Magistrates' Courts Act 1980.

1 Ownership of Wild Animals and Birds

1.1 Introduction

Before one can sensibly explain the current state of the law as to the ownership of the right to take, kill and or shoot game in a particular context, or in relation to a particular area of land, it is necessary to define what one means by the term 'game' (of which more later)[1] but also state how (if at all) a landowner can own the game itself, and explain what right if any the land owner can have at law over the game.

Given that English civil law relies on the establishment of a right and evidence of its infringement in order to found an action, it is first essential to establish what rights exist before going on to see how they might have been infringed. There is also much overlap between the civil and criminal law in this area.

The term 'game' has not been universally defined as a matter of law. It can be seen from the discussion of this issue in Chapter 2 that, whilst the term 'game' is defined in statute,[2] its use in legal drafting for example in connection with conveyancing of rural land is such that the term 'game' means in each case that which it is defined to mean. Because in some circumstances game can mean certain animal species as well and birds both expressions are used in this chapter rather than discussing the position in relation to the legal ownership of birds only.

Unlike the definition of game, the ownership and establishment of property rights over wild animals in general and game species in particular is much easier to describe and explain. Few areas of English law have been settled for as long as the ownership of wild animals and birds. In dealing this area of the law it is necessary, however, in view of the antiquity of the case law to grapple with some ancient legal concepts and thus much legal Latin.

---

[1] See Chapter 2.

[2] Usually inconsistently and differently between statutes.

1.2   Ownership of domestic animals and birds

It has long been settled law that tame or domesticated animals referred to in legal Latin as *mansuetae naturae* can be the subject of property rights in favour of an owner and thus be a chattel. It might be thought that as game birds for example are often reared in captivity before then being released that they could be owned in this way. This indeed is true whilst they remain in captivity[3] but as soon as such birds are allowed to assume a wild state the unqualified ownership that would normally exist in favour of any other 'normal' chattel ceases.

This cessation of rights of ownership over wild birds does not apply to domestic ones in the event of their escape.[4]

1.3   Wild animals or birds

A wild animal may be best described as one falling into one of two categories. These are either, first, an animal which is by disposition fierce (for example a lion) but also, second, an animal which is not tame or domesticated and lives in a wild state, for example a wild game bird. Clearly in this book we are concerned with the second category rather than the first.

The law as to the property rights that one might acquire in respect of wild animals including game (known as *ferae naturae*) has been settled for hundreds of years. It is not often that in considering modern property rights, that reference has to be made to textbooks and case law from several hundred years ago but the law has been settled that long. A discussion of the older cases informs an understanding of the more modern cases. It will be seen from the consideration of the law below that such an examination is essential to understand where the modern law now rests.

The easiest way to explain the modern law in the writer's opinion is to start in the 13th century with the views of Bracton, to then move on from there to a famous case from the 16th century and then examine the case law from later centuries both in respect of civil law and criminal law. There have been practically no significant cases since the Second World War on this issue. Much turns in both the civil and criminal cases, as will be seen as to whether in a particular case a bird or animal could be owned and thus whether a person taking it could commit a crime by

---

[3]   Se *R v Shickle* 1865–72 LR 1 CCR 158, discussed at para 1.5 below.

[4]   See *Hamps v Darby* [1948] 2 KB 311, discussed at para 1.4 below.

doing so. The key sections of the most important cases are reproduced below. The writer considers that other works on this subject make bald assertions on the subject which whilst generally correct do not bring out the nuances of meaning that can only be picked up be reading the original law reports.

By way of an initial summary of the law it will be seen from an examination of the texts and cases that whilst wild animals or birds are not chattels, there exists as a matter of law a series of qualified property rights in wild animals and thus game. These are the right over captured animals reduced into the possession of a human known as property *per industriam*; the right of a landowner over the young of wild animals on his land until such time as they can escape known as *ratione impotentiae et loci*, and the right that a landowner in possession of the sporting rights or an owner possessed of the right of sporting over land[5] has to hunt and take the animals known in the former case as a right *ratione soli* and in the latter as a right *ratione privilgii*. The nature of these rights will be considered in length below.

1.4   Ownership of wild animals per industriam

Bracton in his *De legibus et consuetudinibus Angliae*[6] written it is thought in the 1220s and 1230s states in that part entitled 'How the dominion of things is acquired by the *jus naturale* or the *jus gentium*' the chapter heading being 'Wild Beasts':[7]

> By the *jus gentium* or natural law the dominion of things is acquired in many ways. First by taking possession of things that are owned by no one, and do not now belong to the king by the civil law, no longer being common as before, as wild beasts, birds and fish, that is, all the creatures born on the earth, in the sea or in the heavens, that is, in the air, no matter where they may be taken. When they are captured they begin to be mine, because they are forcibly kept in my custody, and by the same token, if they escape from it and recover their natural liberty they cease to be mine and are again made the property of the taker. They recover their natural liberty when they escape from my sight into the free air and are no longer in my keeping, or when, though still within my view, their pursuit is no longer possible.

---

5   For example a non-freeholder who holds the right to kill or take game, this might be a leaseholder or the holder of a *profit à prendre*.

6   Usually translated as 'On the Laws and Customs of England'.

7   See Harvard Law School library translation.

The book continues, in the next chapter entitled 'Of Fishing, Hunting, and capture', as follows:

> The taking of possession also includes fishing, hunting and capture. It is not pursuit alone that makes a thing mine, for though I have wounded a wild beast so severely that it may be captured, it nevertheless is not mine unless I capture it; rather it will belong to the one who next takes it, for much may happen to prevent my capture of it. And so if a wild boar falls into a net you have set, and though he is caught fast in it I have extricated him and carried him off; he will be mine if he comes into my power, unless custom rules to the contrary or [the king's] privilege.

He deals with the apparent paradox that a wild bird which escapes becomes wild again, whereas a tame bird such as a hen which escapes into the wild does not as follows:

> What has been said applies to animals which always remain wild. But if wild animals are tamed and customarily go and come back, or fly away and return, as deer, peafowl and pigeons, another rule is applicable, namely, that they are taken to be ours so long as they have the intention of returning, for if they cease to have that intention they cease to be ours. They are taken no longer to have the intention of returning when they lose the habit of returning. The same is true of wild hens and wild geese that have become tame. With regard to domestic animals a third rule is applicable, that though they fly out of my view they remain my hens and geese, no matter where they are, and he who takes them with the intention of keeping them commits a theft.

Thus Bracton here deals with and describes the foundation of the concept of qualified ownership in taking animals *per industriam*. This appears to be a right similar to actual unqualified ownership arising from the act of capture taking or taming them which ceases once they assume their wild state. This thus differs from the unqualified right of ownership in domestic animals and birds which persists even after the domesticated animal has escaped. The policy reason for the different treatment of wild and tame or domesticated animals is difficult to fault and it is submitted practical in its utility.

The case of *Grymes v Shack*[8] illustrates this point clearly in a context unconnected with game, namely that an action for the torts of trover (now trespass to goods) and conversion can lie in as the case note says 'Musk cats monkies (sic) and parrots' which were captive and in the possession of the plaintiff thus showing that the key issue is the capture and retention of the wild animal or bird.

---

[8]   (1610) Cro Jac 262.

A more modern statement of the law in relation to qualified ownership showing the different treatment of tame and wild animals so far as property rights is concerned, for example the difficult issue of whether or not racing pigeons can be owned and whether the rules applying to wild animal apply to them is set out in the judgment of Evershed LJ in *Hamps v Darby*.[9] This is a case where the defendant farmer shot the claimant's racing pigeons that were damaging his pea crop and was sued when four of them were killed. If they were wild whilst at large as would be the case with for example pheasants then no action would lie on the principle of title *per industriam* as explained above and the case was defended on that basis by the farmer's advocate. Evershed LJ states:

> It follows, therefore, in our judgment, that the owner of tamed or reclaimed pigeons continues to have property in and possession of his birds after they have flown from his dovecote, so long as the birds retain in fact an animus revertendi to his control. In the present case it was, in our judgment, clearly proved – and the learned county court judge held – that such animus revertendi subsisted in the pigeons which the defendant shot. The plaintiff is, therefore, in our view, entitled *prima facie* to maintain his action in respect of their destruction and wounding.

The position of tame or domestic animals illustrated by *Hamps v Darby* can be contrasted with the limited or nonexistent right over truly wild ones. In *Gott v Measures*[10] a dog was shot by the owner of the sporting rights on land caught by those rights after having been seen tearing a wild pheasant to bits and whilst it was chasing a hare. The issue in the case turned on whether the owner of the sporting rights could reasonably have been protecting his property, in other words did he have any right of ownership in the hare whilst the dog was chasing the hare before it was caught?

Lord Goddard CJ giving the judgment of the Divisional Court said:

> In this case the respondent shot and killed the appellant's dog while it was chasing a hare, and when the dog was about forty yards away from the hare. It is found that he knew it was the appellant's dog and that the appellant had been warned on several occasions about the dog trespassing on land belonging to the respondent. It may be an un-neighbourly act not to keep the dog out, and it was no doubt a very annoying thing for the person who had the sporting rights over the land to find the dog chasing the game which he had the right to shoot. The question remains whether or not in law he was justified in shooting the dog ...

---

[9]   [1948] 2 KB 311.

[10]   [1948] 1 KB 234.

It seems to me that the law really is not in any doubt here, and that is that a person may be justified in shooting a dog if he honestly believes that it is necessary as being the only way in which he can protect his property. Therefore, if a farmer finds a dog driving his ewe flock, as sometimes happens, chasing sheep, and so forth, which may cause incalculable damage to a farmer, it may be that the only way in which he can protect his flock is by shooting the dog, and he can do it. This case is one in which it seems to me the respondent had no property in anything. He had the sporting rights. He, either by leave or licence or by virtue of a grant, was entitled to go on the land for the purpose of hunting game, but he had no property in the game. He had no property in the land and he had no property in the game until he had reduced the game into possession. Neither a person owning the sporting rights nor the landowner has any property in wild game. He has no property in a covey of partridges or in wild pheasants. If he has pheasants in breeding pens, that is another matter, because they are in the same position as domestic fowls, but he has no property in a hare unless and until he has shot the hare and got it.

Therefore, it seems to me that at the time when this occurred it cannot be said that the respondent could have reasonably believed that he was entitled to shoot the dog as being done in protection of his property, because that would be a reasonable belief in something which the law does not recognize. Just as you cannot have a bona fide claim of right if the right is one which the law does not recognize, so it seems to me you cannot honestly believe that it is necessary to shoot a dog to protect your property when you have no property to protect.[11]

As mentioned above the issue of ownership of wild animals is often of relevance in relation to criminal prosecutions.[12] The modern law as to the ownership of a live or dead wild animal or bird is set out in Theft Act 1968, s 4(4) which when enacted replicated the ancient law as to ownership of wild animals described above. It states:

Wild creatures, tamed or untamed, shall be regarded as property; but a person cannot steal a wild creature not tamed nor ordinarily kept in captivity, or the carcase of any such creature, unless either it has been reduced into possession by or on behalf of another person and possession of it has not since been lost or abandoned, or another person is in course of reducing it into possession.

---

11 The effect of this case as to the landowner's belief was reversed by Criminal Damage Act 1971, s 5(3), which reads 'For the purposes of this section it is immaterial whether a belief is justified or not if it is honestly held'.

12 For an ambitious defence of a theft prosecution see *R v Rowland Gallears* [1849] 1 Den 500 where it was argued that as the pork which the defendant had stolen might be wild boar it was not owned and could not be the subject to theft. The defence failed for the obvious reason that a wild animal can be possessed if captured.

There appears to be no case law as to what constitutes 'reducing into possession'. Common sense dictates that this must however consist of putting a carcass into a vehicle or having it about one's person whether or not in a bag. It is not known what the purpose of the first sentence is[13] and how one can regard something as property but it not be capable of being stolen save in circumstances where the law had historically regarded it as property in any event. It is the writer's view that much of the case law in this chapter dealing with allegations against trespassers who committed the former offence of larceny might be differently decided given this section's enactment.

1.5   Ownership of the young of wild animal and birds ratione impotentiae et loci

The established law as to a landowner's title to the young of wild animals in accordance with the principal of *ratione impotentiae et loci* is also ancient. The most famous case covering this area is the *Case of Swans*[14] where the principle issue in hand was the ownership of Swans at Abbotsbury, Dorset. It was held that swans being Royal birds in general belong to the Crown, subject to certain exceptions which are not relevant to the discussion of the law in this book. As will be seen from the quotation from the judgment below in this case the judge Sir Edward Coke takes the opportunity to state the accepted pre-existing law as derived from Bracton and then goes on to build on the historic law in relation to rights over wild animals to suit his own analysis. In reaching a conclusion on the main issue in the case Sir Edward Coke said:

> … there are three manner of rights of property, property absolute, property qualified, and property possessory. A man hath not absolute property in anything which is *ferae naturae*, but in those which are *domitae naturae*.[15]

> Property qualified and possessory a man may have in those which are *ferae naturae*; and to such property a man may attain by two ways, by industry, or *ratione impotentiae et loci* by industry as by taking them, or by making them *mansueta* … But in those which are *ferae naturae*, and by industry are made tame, a man hath but a qualified property in them, so long as they remain tame, for if they do attain to their natural liberty, and have not *animum revertendi*, the property is lost, *ratione impotentiae et loci*.

---

[13]   Ie 'Wild creatures, tamed or untamed, shall be regarded as property'.

[14]   (1592) 7 Co Rep 15b.

[15]   Ie tame or *mansuetae naturae*.

As if a man has young Shovelers or Goshawks, or the like, which are *ferae naturae*, and they build in my land, I have possessory property in them, for if one takes them when they cannot fly, the owner of the soil shall have an action of Trespass, ... But when a man hath savage beasts *ratione privilegii*, as by reason of a Park, Warren, &c. he hath not any property in the Deer, or Conies, or Pheasants, or Partridges, and therefore in an action, ... he shall not say ... for he hath no property in them, but they do belong to him *ratione privilegii* for his game and pleasure, so long as they remain in the privileged place ... nor can Felony be committed of them, but of those which are made tame, in which a man by his industry hath any property, Felony may be committed.

The *Case of Swans* thus is authority for the proposition that the owner of land had title in the young of wild animals and birds which ceases when they are young enough to escape from human pursuers. It also describes as will be seen from the end of the quotation above the issue of the qualified ownership by land owners and their sporting tenants over wild animals on their land at any time.

The case of *R v Shickle*[16] where a thief took young pheasants from a coop confirms[17] first, that there can be property in a tame pheasant, second, that that the young of a pheasant can be owned by the land owner whilst subject to his dominion and thirdly that as a human had title they thus can be stolen.

1.6   Landowners' rights ratione soli or ratione priviligii

The owner of a freehold who retains the sporting or game rights or the owner of those rights to whom they have been transmitted either by lease or as a *profit à prendre* has the unqualified right to take the wild animals on his land[18] and acquires title to animals either live or dead taken by third parties without his permission. The most modern statement of the law on this issue (which also reiterates much of the law on property *per industiam* and *ratione impotentiae et loci*) is the judgment of Lord Westbury C in *Blades v Higgs*.[19] This is often cited when trying to

---

[16]   1865–72 LR 1 CCR 158.

[17]   See in particular judgement of Bovill CJ.

[18]   Although the taking of a number of species either at all or in certain ways, eg with dogs will or may now be illegal, eg foxes, badgers, etc.

[19]   (1865) 29 JP 390.

explain who owns a wild animal or game bird in various circumstances connected with how it came to be reduced into the possession of a particular person. Lord Westbury in this case stated:[20]

(1) If P, a trespasser, start and capture a Hare or wild animal on the soil of A, the property in the animal continues all the while in A, who can recover it by an action of trover.

(2) If P start game in the forest or warren of A, and hunt it into the soil of B, and kill it there, the property also continues in A *ratione privilegii.*

(3) If P start game on the soil of A, and pursue and catch it on the soil of B, then the property is neither in A nor B, but in P, the trespasser.

(4) When it is said that there is a qualified or special right of property in game, that is in animals feræ naturæ which are fit for the food of man, while they continue in their wild state, I apprehend that the word 'property' can mean no more than the exclusive right to catch, kill and appropriate such animals which is sometimes called by the law a reduction of them into possession. This right is said in law to exist *ratione soli*, or *ratione privilegii.*

(5) Property *ratione soli* is the common law right which every owner of land has to kill and take all such animals *feræ naturæ* as may from time to time be found on his land, and as soon as this right is exercised the animal so killed or caught becomes the absolute property of the owner of the soil.

(6) Property *ratione privilegii* is the right which, by a peculiar franchise anciently granted by the Crown in virtue of its prerogative, one man may have of killing and taking animals *feræ naturæ* on the land of another; and in like manner, the game, when killed or taken by virtue of this privilege, becomes the absolute property of the owner of the franchise, just as in the other case it becomes the absolute property of the owner of the soil.

Blades v Higgs thus is authority amongst other things for the proposition that a claim to trespass to goods is maintainable for the young of wild animals or birds taken from a land owner's land. It also confirms and reinforces the position as to property *per industriam* described above and is a useful checklist in trying to work out who owns a wild animal or bird. This put most simply depends on how it came to be taken from its wild state and reduced whether live or dead into the possession of a person.

---

20 The judgment has been often criticised but has never been overruled. It is thought that although the judgment is obviously and manifestly wrong it is unlikely to be overruled.

How can one reconcile the apparent inconsistency in the case law which tends to show both that there is no absolute ownership of wild animals or birds and yet there is a right of ownership vested in the landowner once it has been killed by a non-land- or right-owning third party? It is submitted that the first principle to consider is that there is as a matter of law for very sensible reasons no ownership in any accepted sense of a wild animal or bird. If someone other than the holder of the qualified right to take it kills it, then the act of reducing it into human possession triggers the right either *ratione soli* or *ratione priviligii* such that ownership in the now dead animal passes to the owner of the right. In the writer's view this right is in effect a negative right to be allowed to take or kill wild animals ahead of anyone else and to own the animal if a third party kills or takes it in breach of the land owner's rights. There is no doubt that a landowner owns the carcases of dead animals taken on his land in breach of his rights unless he otherwise agrees.[21] The concept of property *ratione soli* or *ratione priviligii* also forms the basis of the poaching laws which as can be seen from Chapter 7 stand separate from the law of theft. The case law does however show that the courts are prepared to recognise the right either *ratione soli* or *ratione privilgii* as giving rise to ownership rights in wild animals when the animal or birds are severed from the holding on which they reside, even if the act which is alleged to be illegal consists of a series of discontinuous acts.

An example of this discontinuity in the act of reducing into possession is the criminal case of *R v Lewis Townley*[22] where a group of poachers took rabbits from Crown land and parcelled them up in a ditch to be collected some 3 hours later. The issue in the case was one of ownership by the Crown of the rabbits, otherwise as explained in *Gott v Measures* no theft could have been committed. Of course the acts complained of might still amount to poaching.

In the case of *Townley* Bovill CJ stated:

> the first question is as to the nature of the property in these rabbits. In animals *feræ naturæ* there is no absolute property. There is only a special or qualified right of property – a right *ratione soli* to take and kill them. When killed upon the soil they become the absolute property of the owner of the soil. This was decided in the case of rabbits by the House of Lords in *Blade v. Higgs*. And the same principle was applied in the case of grouse in *Lord Lonsdale v. Rigg*. In this case therefore the rabbits, being started and killed on land belonging to the Crown, might, if there were no other circumstance in

---

[21]   See *Fitzgerald v Firbank* [1897] 2 CH 96, CA.

[22]   1865–72 LR 1 CCR 315.

the case, become the property of the Crown. But before there can be a conviction for larceny for taking anything not capable in its original state of being the subject of larceny, as for instance, things fixed to the soil it is necessary that the act of taking away should not be one continuous act with the act of severance or other act by which the thing becomes a chattel, and so is brought within the law of larceny. This doctrine has been applied to stripping lead from the roof of a church, and in other cases of things affixed to the soil. And the present case must be governed by the same principle.

1.7   The relationship between the tort of trespass and ownership of wild animals and birds

Although as is explained above somewhat bizarrely there exist circumstances in which a trespasser can acquire title to a wild animal that he kills on land belonging to another[23] this will not avoid an action for the tort of trespass against such a trespasser for entering onto the land of the landowner without licence or consent. Such an entry clearly constitutes an unlawful entry onto land in the possession of another and thus the elements of the tort are satisfied.

In addition such entry may contravene several statutes and in particular Game Act 1831 (GA 1831), s 30 which creates the offence of entering land in the daytime in pursuit of game. There is a similar offence created in respect of entering in the night time.[24]

As stated above, taking game at certain times of the week or year[25] is illegal as may be taking some wild species in all circumstances. GA 1831, s 46 preserves the landowner's right to pursue an action for trespass against one who trespasses in pursuit of game on his land, but eliminates the double jeopardy to the offender who does trespass in pursuit of game by preventing any action for trespass where the offender is prosecuted under the GA 1831 for any of the offences created by that statute involving trespass in pursuit of game.

---

[23]   See eg the third circumstance cited by Lord Westbury C in *Blades v Higgs*, at para 16.2.

[24]   Eg the Night Poaching Act 1824 and subsequent poaching statutes.

[25]   See discussion of closed seasons in Chapter 6.

Section 46 states:

> **46 This Act not to preclude actions for trespass, but no double proceedings for the same trespass**
>
> Provided always, that nothing in this Act contained shall prevent any person from proceeding by way of civil action to recover damages in respect of any trespass upon his land, whether committed in pursuit of game or otherwise, save and except that where any proceedings shall have been instituted under the provisions of this Act against any person for or in respect of any trespass, no action at law shall be maintainable for the same trespass by any person at whose instance or with whose concurrence or assent such proceedings shall have been instituted, but that such proceedings shall in such case be a bar to any such action.

Note that the only offences which are relieved from a civil action are those under the GA 1831 and not for example under the various Poaching Prevention Acts or the Wildlife and Countryside Act 1981 (WCA 1981).

1.8   Anomalous cases relating to the right to take birds

There are two apparently incongruous older cases both sharing similar facts which are worthy of examination at this point. Both relate to a situation where a person attracts wild birds onto his land with a view to killing or taking them and then at the hand of a neighbour suffers having the wild birds scared away by the neighbour discharging a weapon. In both cases the land owner sought damages for his loss from the neighbour who had discharged the weapon.

In *Keeble v Hickeringill*,[26] a case from 1706, the claimant had a duck pond on his property and alleged that the defendant fired guns on his property for the purposes of scaring away the wild duck from the pond. He did not enter onto the claimant's property and the claimant could not say how many ducks had been scared away. In holding that these facts gave rise to a right of action for injury and the enjoyment of a profitable piece of property without the claimant having to prove how many ducks he had lost, Sir John Holt CJ said in his judgment: '... the true reason is, that this action is not brought to recover damages for loss of the fowl but for the disturbance'.

In other words he was stating that this was not a claim to a loss of property but a claim in effect for what would now be the tort of nuisance.

---

[26]   [1558–1774] All ER Rep 286.

The contrasting case is that of *Hannan v Mockett*[27] a century or so later from 1824 where the claimant alleged that he was the owner of land on which trees were growing, in which rooks had been used to settle and build their nests. The claimant had been used to killing them, taking the rooks (presumably for eating) and alleged that the defendant had wrongfully and maliciously caused guns loaded with gunpowder to be discharged near the trees so that they were driven away. The court in taking a completely different view from that which had been adopted in *Keeble v Hickeringill*, which it found it could distinguish, found that wild fowl were a known article of food and 'that a person keeping up a decoy expends money and employs skill in taking that which is of use to the public. It is a profitable mode of employing his land ...'. The judgment continues, as follows:

> upon the ground therefore that the plaintiff had no property in these rooks, that they are birds *ferae naturae*, destructive in their habits and not protected either by common law statute and that the plaintiff is at no expense with regard to them, we are of the opinion that the plaintiff has no right to insist on them in his neighbourhood and he cannot maintain this action.

Were either or both of these actions to be considered in a modern context it is likely that they would be pursued as a nuisance action (whether public or private will depend upon the extent of the unpleasantness caused by the discharge of the guns). These cases serve to show if anything the development of the forms of action from the action on the case being employed in both of these actions to the modern forms of action which now can be brought before the courts.

1.9   Ancient prerogative rights of the Crown

Prior to the enactment of the Wild Creatures and Forest Laws Act 1971 it was possible to possess a right over the land of another to kill and take game and other species by virtue of a right of franchise granted by the Crown. Section 1 of this Act abolished such rights together with the ancient right of chase warren and free warren that so obsessed lawyers in previous ages. The statute reads:

(1) There are hereby abolished—

  (a) any prerogative right of Her Majesty to wild creatures (except royal fish and swans), together with any prerogative right to set aside land or water for the breeding, support or taking of wild creatures; and

  (b) any franchises of forest, free chase, park or free warren.

---

[27]   [1824] 2 B&C 934.

The Act thus preserves the ancient Crown rights over whales, sturgeon and swans. This Act does not however affect the rights of a lord of the manor to game under the *ratione priveligii* principle discussed above over waste land of the manor which is unenclosed.

1.10   Summary

The law in relation to the ownership of wild animals and birds can thus it is submitted be reduced to the following propositions:

• One can own domestic animals and title to such animals apparently cannot be lost even if they escape into the wild whilst they remain domesticated.

• One cannot own wild animals until they are captured.

• Once captured one can own a wild animal.

• If they escape from an owner, wild animals become ownerless and subject to being reduced into the possession of another person who can in some circumstances acquire title to the animals.

• Dead wild animals and birds belong absolutely to the landowner on whose land they die.

• The young of wild animals and birds belong to the landowner on whose land they sit until such time as they are old enough to escape.

• The owner of land (or the right to take and kill wild animals and bird on the land if not the freehold owner) has the right to take and kill wild animals and birds and to the extent that another does so without his permission they commit the civil wrong of trespass to goods and also potentially several criminal offences.

• Entering in pursuit of game may lead to one acquiring title in the game but may still lead to one being at risk of an action for trespass from the owner of the land or sporting rights on whose land the game is taken.

2 Game and its Various Meanings and Definitions

2.1 Introduction

There are in the writer's opinion two issues to consider when trying to ascertain the meaning of the word 'game' as a matter of law. First, how is it used in the many statutes which regulate the law of shooting and game? Second, how is it used in private arrangements between the owners of land, those who shoot the land (if different) and the tenants or other occupier of the land?

A table showing which creatures (being certain species of game birds together with rabbits and hares) are defined as game in the principal statutes currently still in force is set out below (see Table 2.1).

Table 2.1: Creatures defined as game in the principal statutes still in force

Statute	*GA 1831*	*GGA 1880*	*NPA 1828*	*PPA 1862*	*GLAA 1960*	*WCA 1981*	*AHA 1986*[1]
Section number	2	8	13	1	4(5)	27	20
Pheasants	Yes	No	Yes	Yes	Yes	Yes	Yes
Partridges	Yes	No	Yes	Yes	Yes	Yes	Yes
Grouse[2]	Yes	No	Yes	Yes	Yes	Yes	Yes
Heath/moor game[3]	Yes	No	Yes	Yes	Yes	N/A	Yes

---

[1]   As long as the right to kill or take the species in question is vested in the landlord or one deriving title under him, see AHA 1986, s 20(1).

[2]   Grouse includes several species – both red and black game are grouse, see later in para 2.1 at page 16 for a discussion of this issue.

[3]   Ie the red grouse (*lagopus lagopus scotica*).

Statute	GA 1831	GGA 1880	NPA 1828	PPA 1862	GLAA 1960	WCA 1981	AHA 1986[1]
Section number	2	8	13	1	4(5)	27	20
Black game[4]	Yes	No	Yes	Yes	Yes	Yes	Yes
Hares	Yes	Yes	Yes	Yes	Yes	No	Yes
Rabbits	Yes	Yes	No	Yes	No	No	Yes
Bustards[5]	No	No	Yes		Yes	No	Yes
Woodcock	No	No	No	Yes	Yes	No	Yes
Snipe	No	No	No	Yes	Yes	No	Yes
Ptarmigan	No	No	No	No	No	Yes	Yes

It will be noted that there is some confusion between parliamentary draftsmen as to the difference between heath or moor game and black game. The former is the red grouse (*lagopus lagopus scotica*) the latter is the black grouse (*tetrao tetrix*). The Poaching Prevention Act 1862 (PPA 1862) seems to define it as black or moor game which might mean that one is the synonym of the other or that the draftsman wanted to refer to both. The writer suspects the erroneous first option is correct.[6]

In addition, the term grouse which is used in all of the statutes except the Ground Game Act 1880 (GGA 1880) is a reference to a number of species which now include the red and black grouse. The species include the following genus and species[7] which are the only species found in the United Kingdom (see Table 2.2). It is not thought that the capercaillie which is now extremely rare is likely to be shot by any responsible sportsman. It is found now in the Highlands of Scotland only, so English law is of little relevance to it.

---

[4]   Ie the black grouse (*tetrao tetrix*).

[5]   Bustards were hunted out of existence in Britain by the 1840s. There is a project to reintroduce them to the United Kingdom in progress at present.

[6]   This problem is not unique to this statute, eg in Wild Birds Act 1967, s 8(4) (now repealed) 'wild bird' was defined as including grouse (or moor game) and black (or heath game).

[7]   See British Ornithological Union official UK list, available at www.bou.org.uk/recbrlst1.html.

Table 2.2: Species and genus of grouse

Species common name	Also known as	Latin name
Red grouse	Willow ptarmigan	*Lagopus lagopus*
Ptarmigan	Rock ptarmigan	*Lagopus muta*
Black grouse		*Tetrao tetrix*
Capercaillie		*Tetrao urogallus*

Several statutes include the bustard, which was extinct in England shortly after the earliest of those statutes was drafted and the shooting of which would not now be permitted by the WCA 1981.[8]

Several species regularly shot by sportsmen on private and commercial shoots are not included in most of the statutes although may be included in some of the sections by way of an addition to the term game.[9] The category mentioned here will for example include the snipe, ptarmigan, woodcock and guinea fowl. All wild fowl (ducks, geese, etc) are excluded. Similar protection will be afforded to these species by the WCA 1981 or by other statutes but the position is messy and inconsistent. This largely arises from the antiquity of the statutes and the change in shooting practices over the years.

Some statutes, for example the GA 1831, use a definition which is such that the definition 'includes' and is then followed by a list. It might be though that this list is thus illustrative of the creatures which are within and that others might be included, but the writer's view is that the word 'includes' should be ignored and that the list should be construed as if it were conclusive.

There is an inconsistency in definition between statutes on the same subject, for example the Night Poaching Act 1828 (NPA 1828) and PPA 1862 (snipe), and the different definition used in the GA 1831 and the Game Laws (Amendment) Act 1960 (GLAA 1960), which amends the former and also includes reference to the bustard which by the time of its enactment had been extinct in England since c 1840.[10]

---

[8] For an update on the project to reintroduce this bird to the United Kingdom, see www.greatbustard.com.

[9] See eg GA 1831, ss 31 and 32, which adds woodcock snipe and conies (rabbits) to game for the purposes of those sections.

[10] Things have been improved by the passing of the Regulatory Reform (Game) Order 2007. The statutes which were repealed by it contained even more inconsistent definitions.

Although hares have been included in some statutes in the definition of game, one should not confuse game with ground game. The former consist of any species defined by statute as being the subject of sport, whereas the latter are in effect vermin[11] that an occupier of land can cull to prevent crop damage.

It will be noted that deer and indeed fish are not included in the statutes although can be included in private grants of rights.[12]

In summary, therefore, the whole area of the definition of 'game' is a mess with no easy answer for the researcher who will need to consider the whole statute or a number of statutes before being able to understand what is meant by game in a particular context. This could so easily have been avoided if at the time that the Regulatory Reform (Game) Order 2007[13] (RRO 2007) had been passed, instead of an RRO time had been found for a Game Laws Act 2007. The position is by no means unique in relation to the law of the countryside, for example there is no consistent definition of 'agriculture' or 'livestock' in relevant statutes.

The position in relation to the definition of game in general use or legal documents is very different. There appear to be no universal definitions or common usage. In effect, in this context game means whatever it is defined to mean.

Three cases illustrate the approach the courts have used over the past 200 years in defining what is 'game' for the purposes of its meaning in legal documents. The oldest of these, *Moore v Earl of Plymouth*[14] from 1817, confirms that an exception in a conveyance to the landowner of 'the free liberty of hawking and hunting' does not include the ability to shoot feathered game with a gun. This case is authority for the proposition that in each case the draftsman needs to craft and define exactly what he or she is wishing the recipient of the grant to receive.

In *Jeffryes v Evans*[15] by contrast a much wider definition had been used namely 'the right of shooting and sporting' over the land. It was held that this grant was not limited to game strictly so-called but reserved to the lessor the exclusive right to follow and shoot such animals as are generally understood in common parlance to be the subject of sport.

---

[11]   Limited to hares and rabbits.

[12]   See the case of *Inglewood Investment Company Ltd v Forestry Commissioners* [1988] 1 WLR 1278, discussed below.

[13]   SI 2007/2007.

[14]   (1817) 7 Taunt 614.

[15]   (1865) 19 CBNS 246.

An example of drafting which clearly went wrong for the purposes of the tenant getting what he wanted is the more modern case of *Inglewood Investment Company Ltd v Forestry Commissioners*[16] where a 1921 lease to the Forestry Commission reserved to the freeholders 'all game, woodcocks, snipe and other wild fowl, hares, rabbits and fish'. The claimants brought proceedings seeking a declaration from the Commission that the Commission was not entitled to hunt or take any deer from the land on the basis that deer were within the terms 'all game' and were therefore preserved. Harman J at first instance held that in construing the particular reservation one had to take account of the circumstances of usage as existed at the date of grant. Following this analysis the definition of 'game' depended on the defined context of 'woodcocks, snipe and wild fowl' and thus did not include deer. In giving judgment of the Court of Appeal Dillon LJ said:

> looking at it in the context of the present case what is immediately apparent is that the word 'game' has been used in collocation with woodcocks, snipe and other wild fowl, hares, rabbits and fish. Had deer been in the mind of the draftsman of the clause I have no doubt it would have been mentioned. It is conspicuous by its absence. I find it therefore impossible to construe the word 'game' as including deer in the context where the draftsman has set out a list of other birds and animals to which the clause is to apply and which it might not be clear were definitely covered by the word 'game'. That is to say woodcocks, snipe and other wild fowl, hares, rabbits and fish. The clause has obviously been professionally drawn but has not been identified as coming from any particular established precedent book. It is a clause which may have served its purpose reasonably well for many years but has not been able to pass without criticism on all sides when it became necessary to apply it in circumstances which as it seems to me were outside the contemplation of the draftsman.

It will therefore be important for any draftsman who is seeking to bring a particular species within or without the contemplation of a clause to mention it expressly in the terms of the grant or suffer uncertainty and thus litigation risk when the document comes to be argued over in court.

---

[16]   [1988] 1 WLR 1278.

2.2   Summary

- The definitions of 'game' in relevant statutes are incongruent and contradictory. There is no substitute for considering the definition in each case and there is no short cut to ascertaining what each statute defines 'game' to mean.

- In respect of the term 'game' in drafting legal documents, it means what it is defined to mean.

- As guidance to those involved in drafting a grant of sporting rights it is wise to make the grant as wide as possible; just reserving the right to 'hawk and hunt' will not allow shooting, and deer need to be expressly reserved as they are not game.

3 The Game Act 1831

3.1 Introduction and history

The principal statute regulating the taking and killing of game birds[1] in England and Wales is the GA 1831. This statute was revolutionary at the time it was passed insofar as it ensured that, for the first time since the Norman Conquest, there was a separation of the taking and killing of game birds from the ownership of a certain value of land.

After the GA 1831, subject to possession of a game licence and the permission of the holder of the right to enter onto the land for the purposes of killing or taking the game, anyone could engage in the sport of game shooting or taking game by other means. The possession of a game licence was at the core of the legislation and the right to shoot game was intrinsically linked to the possession of such a licence. As can be seen below, the consensus established by the GA 1831 has been very much disturbed by the changes brought about by the RRO 2007.

To put the 1831 Act into its context, royalty and the aristocracy had long taken an interest in killing game and hunting. Both were activities reserved to the nobility. At the time of Richard II in the 14th century, no one was entitled to kill game unless qualified by the ownership of sufficient land or social standing. The qualification was raised from a 40 shilling freehold in 1389 to an interest in land falling short of a freehold worth £100 a year or a freehold of £150 by the end of the 17th century. It is clear that the intention behind the GA 1831 was to sever the link with land ownership whilst making it expensive to shoot game (by virtue of the cost of a game licence) and thus preserve it for the upper classes.

3.2 Regulatory Reform (Game) Order 2007

The GA 1831 had been constantly amended and parts of the Act have been repealed and other parts modified almost since its passing. The most major change to the game laws in general and the GA 1831 in particular was enacted by the RRO 2007.

---

[1] Defined for the purposes of this statute only in GA 1831, s 2, this is not to be taken as a general and universal definition of game.

Before the amendments brought about by the RRO 2007, the DEFRA junior Minister at the time of the passage of the Order, Lord Geoff Rooker described the purpose of the game laws somewhat amusingly as preventing 'peasants killing pheasants'. This to a great extent is true because as originally enacted the cost of a game licence was so high as to in reality prevent all but the rich from shooting or taking game species.[2] Over time successive governments failed to up rate the cost of a game licence such that by the late 20th century the costs of collection of the game licence outweighed the revenue collected. It is a shame that, at the same time as modernising the law in relation to game licensing, steps were not taken to modernise the whole law relating to game and sporting generally. It was much easier however to find time for the passage of an RRO (in respect of which there are strict requirements as to what can be done, in the writer's experience policed vigorously by parliamentary counsel), rather than find time for the primary legislation such modernisation would have demanded. The purpose of the RRO 2007 was expressed in the regulatory impact statement issued with it when it was published as 'To remove unnecessary economic and administrative burdens on the killing, taking and dealing in game in England and Wales'. This it certainly achieves.

The RRO 2007 has abolished in England and Wales (but not in Scotland or Northern Ireland where the requirement still persists) all requirements which were previously contained in the GA 1831 and the Game Licensing Act 1860 that a person killing or taking game (save in some special circumstances) had to have a licence to kill game. As a consequence of this fundamental change to the arrangements put in place in 1831, it thus abolishes all the previously existing rules as to who was entitled to stop a person found on a particular parcel of land for the purposes of inspecting their game licence. It also repeals a number of statutes including the Game Licensing Act 1860, the Hares Act 1848 (the effect of which was in any event largely replicated by the GGA 1880) and the Deer Act 1991 (DA 1991). The requirement to have a game licence had been honoured in the breach by much of the shooting community, and the value of the revenue gained from having a game licensing regime had declined with time as successive governments failed to keep up the cost of acquiring such a licence in line with inflation.

---

[2]   According to the parliamentary report on the RRO 2007, the cost of a game
       licence was the equivalent of £1600 at modern prices.

3.3 Game Act 1831 – post-reform

Post the RRO 2007 the GA 1831 now deals with and regulates four elements of game law, namely:

- the days of the week and year on which game can be killed, the closed seasons for taking game and controls over taking the eggs of game (ss 3, 3A and 24);

- the rights to take game during open seasons and the 'ownership' of game (ss 7 to 12);

- the appointment of and powers of gamekeepers by lords of the manor (ss 13 to 16); and

- a number of criminal offences for wrongfully taking game (ss 30 to 36 and 41).

In considering the regulation of the taking or killing a number of species not regulated by the GA 1831 but commonly the subject of sport, reference has to be made in addition to the GA 1831 to the WCA 1981 which is explored more fully in Chapter 6.

The GA 1831 cannot therefore be considered a complete code; the times of the year when some species can be taken are not regulated by the GA 1831 as a result of its antiquity and the changes in the species taken for sport since its enactment. To understand the law fully, reference has to be made to a number of statutes and the case law applying to them to understand the law regulating the killing and taking to what might be called game species in its widest sense.

3.4 Game Act 1831, ss 3, 3A and 24 – introduction

By way of brief introduction, ss 3, 3A and 24 control the time or times during which game birds can legitimately be taken and, in the case of s 24, control the ability of third parties to remove eggs from the nests of certain birds including game birds (as defined in GA 1831, s 2) and others.

3.5 Game Act 1831, s 3

Section 3 remains largely as originally passed. It has not been substantially amended save to replace the fines originally set out in the text with scale fines in accordance with the reorganisation of criminal fines by the Criminal Justice Act 1982. The section creates seven separate criminal offences most of which relate to closed seasons for killing and taking game. For convenience these are not all enumerated and described in this chapter as six of them are dealt more conveniently in Chapter 6 on closed seasons.[3] The one exception is the prohibition contained in s 3 on using poison to kill game. This reads:

> … and if any person, with intent to destroy or injure any game, shall at any time put or cause to be put any poison or poisonous ingredient on any ground, whether open or inclosed, where game usually resort, or in any highway, every such person shall, on conviction thereof before two justices of the peace, forfeit and pay such sum of money, not exceeding level 1 on the standard scale, as to the said justices shall seem meet.

3.6 Game Act 1831, s 3A – selling illegally taken game birds

The purpose of the inclusion of this section was to replace s 4 which was repealed by the RRO 2007 with a new offence of selling, offering or exposing for sale, possessing or transporting for the purposes of sale any game bird that has been killed or taken in contravention of the legislation listed in the new s 3A(2), where the person concerned knows, or has reason to believe, it had been so taken or killed. For completeness the whole section is set out below. It reads:

3A Sale of birds of game

If any person

    (a) Sells or offers or exposes for sale, or

    (b) has in his possession or transports for the purposes of sale, any bird of game to which this subsection applies, he shall be guilty of an offence and liable on summary conviction to a fine not exceeding level 5 on the standard scale or to imprisonment for a term not exceeding six months or to both.

Subsection (1) applies to any bird of game—

    (a) which has been taken or killed in circumstances which constitute an offence under any of—

        (i) the Night Poaching Act 1828;

        (ii) this Act;

        (iii) the Poaching Prevention Act 1862; or

---

[3]   See para 6.5.

(iv) Part 1 of the Wildlife and Countryside Act 1981 (wildlife); and

(b) which the person concerned knows or has reason to believe has been so taken or killed.

Despite diligent searching there appears to be no reported cases on this relatively new section and no prosecutions are known of under it. The terms used in the section will be familiar to those experienced in criminal law, for example 'sells or offers for sale' and 'has in possession', and if any point arises on them it may be best to refer to established criminal textbooks rather than reconsider those phrases here. The only controversy in the drafting of this section in the writer's view is the use of the words 'bird of game' instead of game. Does this intend to imply a wider meaning of the birds covered than 'game' as defined by GA 1831, s 2? The writer's view is that game is most likely to be defined in this section as defined in s 2 to avoid inconsistency, but the wording will remain unclear until a case clarifies this drafting inconsistency.

3.7   Game Act 1831, s 24 – taking eggs of game and other species

Section 24 criminalises the actions of persons who do not have the right of killing game upon any land (in respect of which see Chapter 4) nor having permission of the person having such right who wilfully take eggs of any game birds, swan, wild duck, teal or widgeon or being in possession or control of such eggs. The person breaching this section is liable to a fine at level 1 on the standard scale. It is likely that this section has cross-overs at least so far as the species concerned are not 'game'[4] as defined in GA 1831, s 2 with WCA 1981, s 1(1)(c).[5] Given the penalties under WCA 1981, ss 1 to 13 are up to a level 5 fine, whereas the penalty under GA 1831, s 24 is a level 1 fine, it is not surprising that the section is seldom if ever now used by prosecutors; if they can use the WCA 1981 they will do so although, as can be seen below, they cannot do so in respect of game species as defined by GA 1831, s 2 because such species are not caught by the WCA 1981.

A constable may also rely on WCA 1981, s 19 to legitimately seize eggs and also has powers to seize chattels including eggs generally under Police and Criminal Evidence Act 1984, s 19.

---

[4]   Game birds are not protected by the WCA 1981 in the same way as other species, see Chapter 6.

[5]   See Chapter 6.

It should be noted that this section also regulates the taking of eggs of species not defined under GA 1831, s 2 as game including swan, wild duck, teal or widgeon; all of these are caught by the WCA 1981 in the definition of 'wild bird'. The full offence also includes destroying the nests of such birds. The section reads:

Penalty for destroying or taking the Eggs of Game, etc

> If any person not having the right of killing the game upon any land, nor having permission from the person having such right, shall wilfully take out of the nest or destroy in the nest upon such land the eggs of any bird of game, or of any swan, wild duck, teal, or widgeon, or shall knowingly have in his house, shop, possession, or control any such eggs so taken, every such person shall, on conviction thereof before two justices of the peace, forfeit and pay for every egg so taken or destroyed, or so found in his house, shop, possession, or control, such sum of money, not exceeding level 1 on the standard scale, as to the said justices shall seem meet.

There is one reported case of importance in relation to s 24, which shows that there are distinct limitations on the use of this section by virtue of the fact that it gives power to summons a person who is allegedly in contravention of what it prescribes but not to seize the eggs in that person's possession.

In *Stowe v Benstead and Another*,[6] a police officer seized some partridge eggs purportedly relying on PPA 1862, s 2 but then took out a summons against the person from whom he seized them charging him with an offence under GA 1831, s 24 which, as can be seen from the wording set out above, contains no power of seizure. It is not known why he did this. In considering what to do in this set of circumstance Darling J said:

> I am of the opinion that as the Police Sergeant instead of proceeding under the Act of 1862 took proceedings under the Act of 1831 which gave him no power to seize the eggs he cannot be allowed to say that he had a right to seize them because he might have seized them if he had been proceeding under the Act of 1862.

Thus the flaws in the section in practice are exposed; it allows a prosecution but no confiscation until after conviction. The powers under the WCA 1981, at least in relation to non-game species, are much more extensive, and in reality this section is now thus redundant in respect of them and little used in respect of game as defined in the WCA 1981 as a result of the limited sanction that a level 1 fine provides.

---

[6]   [1909] 2 KB 415.

3.8   Game Act 1831, ss 7 to 12 – rights over game

These sections provided the framework for the reform of the law post-1831. They also attempted when passed to provide rules as to by whom and if so how the right to kill and take game will be enjoyed post the reform brought in by the Act. As can be seen from the analysis below, much of this part of the Act is archaic and, as it was enacted before the property law reforms brought in by the 1925 legislation. It is thus to an extent superseded by the more wide-ranging reforms of property law which followed.

Section 7 provides that in respect of any existing leases made before the GA 1831 came into force on 5 October 1831, the power to kill game will be reserved to the landlord except in certain specified circumstances. Those circumstances are:

- where the rights of killing the game on the land has been expressly granted or allowed to such person (the tenant) by a lease or agreement for a lease; or

- where on the original granting or renewal of a lease, a fine or fines shall have been taken;[7] and

- where in the case of a lease it has been made for a term exceeding 21 years.

It is unlikely in practice that there are many, if any, leases from before 1831 which are still in force and therefore this explanation is included for completeness.

Section 7 should be read in conjunction with s 8, which provides that nothing in the Act authorises any person who is possessed of any land to kill the game in any circumstance where the rights have been reserved to the grantor or landlord. This is a matter of common sense and practice in any event.

Other works[8] consider that these two sections provide in effect for a situation where post-1831 the landlord must reserve the rights or they will automatically pass to the tenant. It is submitted by the writer that ss 7 and 8 do nothing of the sort but that this outcome arises in any event under the general law. In a leasehold situation where exclusive possession is being given by the landlord to the tenant as must be the

---

[7]   A fine or fines in this context means a premium or a capital payment.

[8]   For example *Oke's Game Laws* (Butterworths, 5th edn, 1912).

case in order to satisfy the long established preconditions for the creation of a lease, if a landlord fails to reserve the rights to kill or take all or any species of game they must pass by implication with the grant of the land because the landlord has no power of access to the land reserved back to him to exercise the right to kill or take game not specifically reserved to himself. In contrast to the leasehold position it is certainly true that in a freehold situation where a *profit à prendre* is being reserved out of the freehold to another party that if a particular species is not mentioned as being granted to that party it will be reserved back to the freeholder. GA 1831, ss 7 and 8, however, only apply to persons who are in occupation or seized of a holding and to landlords who are out of possession.

Sections 9 and 10 are somewhat obscure. Section 9 provides that nothing in the Act affects the prerogative rights or privileges of the Crown. These, however, have in any event been severely altered and curtailed or event possibly extinguished by the Crown Estate Act 1961 and the Wild Creatures and Forest Laws Act 1971. A discussion of Crown rights to game is set out in Chapter 1, and such limited rights as may exist are in practice not exercised.

Section 10 is even more obscure and is worth quoting in full. The section as amended by the RRO 2007 reads:

> Provided also, that nothing herein contained shall be deemed to give to any owner of cattlegates or rights of common upon or over any wastes or commons any interest or privilege which such owner was not possessed of before the passing of this Act, nor to authorize such owner of cattlegates or rights of common to pursue or kill the game found on such wastes or commons; and that nothing herein contained shall defeat or diminish the rights or privileges which any lord of any manor, lordship, or royalty, or reputed manor, lordship, or royalty, or any steward of the crown of any manor, lordship, or royalty appertaining to his Majesty, may, before the passing of this Act, have exercised in or over such wastes or commons; and that the lord or steward of the crown of every manor, lordship, or royalty, or reputed manor, lordship, or royalty, shall have the right to pursue and kill the game upon the wastes or commons within such manor, lordship, or royalty, or reputed manor, lordship, or royalty, and to authorize any other person or persons to enter upon such wastes or commons for the purpose of pursuing and killing the game thereon.

A cattlegate is an ancient term for a stinted right of common.[9] Usually, it is a right to graze one horned beast but the numbers of animals stinted can be adjusted. In some areas a cattlegate gave the right to graze as

---

[9]   Ie a right which has been defined in terms of number of beasts allowed to graze a defined area.

many as 15 sheep. All this extremely terse text does is to explain that the Act does not provide for owners of cattle gates or rights of common to have the shooting or sporting rights. It is submitted that these rights would have had significantly more practical implication in 1831 than they do now. It can be seen from the wording of this section the importance attached at the time to the rights and privileges of lords of the manor such that their rights needed to be expressly set out when the Act was drafted.

3.9   Game Act 1831, s 11

Section 11 of the Act allows a landlord who has reserved to himself the right of killing and taking the game to authorise other persons to enter upon the land for the purposes of pursuing and killing game. This probably now is implied as a matter of law, but under the pre-1925 reform of land law was not so at the time of the enactment of the Act in 1831.

3.10   Game Act 1831, s 12

Section 12 builds on this section by providing that in a situation where the tenant or the legal occupier of the land does not have the game rights and the tenant or occupier then seeks to exercise them himself or purports to authorise another to do so, he and or they shall be liable for pursuing killing or taking any game on the land and commits a criminal offence and is liable on conviction to a fine of level 1 on the standard scale and for every head of game killed a further fine of level 1 on the standard scale. This section needs to be considered with the discussion of the offences created by ss 30 to 32 below.

3.11   Game Act 1831, s 13 to 16 – gamekeepers

Sections 13 to 16 deal with the powers of gamekeepers appointed by a lord of a manor. These powers have been grossly curtailed by the removal from the GA 1831 of the sections dealing with game licensing. Previously, the greater part of a gamekeeper's function was to check whether people found on private land shooting or sporting on a particular parcel of that land had the requisite game licences in accordance with the policy of the GA 1831 to replace a property qualification to be allowed to shoot with a licensing qualification.

Section 13 allows a lord of a manor, lordship or royalty or any steward of the Crown of any manor, lordship or royalty under hand and seal (which the writer submits means by deed) or in the case of a body corporate under the seal of the company (again by deed[10]) to appoint one or more person(s) as gamekeeper to preserve or kill the game within the limits of the manor. Before the RRO 2007 came into force the section also continued with further text which empowered gamekeepers to inspect game licences and seize or take all dogs, nets and other engines in the killing or taking of game on the holding. This part of the section has now been repealed.

Section 14 builds on the previous section insofar as it provides in somewhat archaic terms for the same parties, ie lords of the manor, lordship or royalty to appoint as their deputy and authorise him to kill game for his own use or for the use of any other person who may be specified in the appointment or deputation and to give him all powers given to a gamekeeper. This is notwithstanding the fact that he might be the servant of another. There appears to be no limit on the number of deputies who might be appointed.

Section 15 makes special regulations for the appointment of gamekeepers in Wales. The reason why Wales is treated separately and differently from England is because historically most of the lordships of the manor in Wales were held by the Crown, whereas in England they were not. This provides, to quote from the section:

> It shall be lawful for every person who shall be entitled to kill the game upon any lands in Wales of the clear annual value of five hundred pounds, whereof he shall be seised in fee or as of freehold, or to which he shall otherwise be beneficially entitled in his own right, if such lands shall not be within the bounds of any manor, lordship, or royalty, or if, being within the same, they shall have been enfranchised or alienated therefrom, to appoint, by writing under his hand and seal, a gamekeeper or gamekeepers to preserve or kill the game over and upon such his lands, and also over and upon the lands in Wales of any other person, who, being entitled to kill the game upon such last-mentioned lands, shall by licence in writing authorize him to appoint a gamekeeper or gamekeepers to preserve or kill the game thereupon, such last-mentioned lands not being within the bounds of any manor, lordship, or royalty, or having been enfranchised or alienated therefrom.

---

[10]   The requirement for a validly executed deed no longer require execution under seal, see Law of Property (Miscellaneous Provisions) Act 1989, s 1(3) and the Regulatory Reform (Execution of Deeds and Documents) Order 2005 (SI 2005/1906).

There is no explanation in the Act as to what the annual value of £500 means but it is submitted that this is more likely to be construed as rateable value rather than open market letting value. The other mechanisms provided for by this section, for example the appointment of a gamekeeper under hand and seal, are the same as in the previous section.

Apart from the decline in the relevance of lordships of the manor in modern times, a further reason why GA 1831, ss 13 to 15 inclusive are probably not of particular importance in the modern age is that by virtue of GA 1831, s 16, no appointment or deputation of any person as a gamekeeper under the GA 1831 is valid unless it is registered with:

> the Clerk of the Peace for the county, riding, division, liberty, franchise, city or town wherein the manor, lordship or royalty or reputed manor, lordship or royalty on the land shall be situate for or in respect of which such person shall have been appointed gamekeeper.

Courts Act 1971, s 44(1)(a) abolished the position of Clerk of the Peace. By virtue of Sch 8 to the same Act any reference to a Clerk of the Peace in another statute is now to be read as a reference to the 'Appropriate Officer of the Crown Court'. This officer is in the writer's view the Clerk to the Crown Court.

The writer has made enquiries of The Crown' Courts Clerks society during the course of preparing this work, and has found that they are not aware of any gamekeeper being appointed under these sections for some time. Whilst the right to register is still notionally available perhaps through lack of knowledge of the availability of the process or a lack of need of the benefits that registration bring this part of the GA 1831 has fallen into disuse.

3.12   Wrongfully taking game and trespass in pursuit of game

GA 1831, ss 30 to 32 create three criminal offences which, unlike much of the GA 1831, are still of relevance in modern times in that there have been a significant number of prosecutions under those sections historically and they still appear to be used occasionally by prosecutors currently. They are, therefore, worth examining in some detail together with the requisite case law.

3.13   Game Act 1831, s 30

By way of introduction, GA 1831, s 30 creates two offences of trespassing in the daytime in search of game (although it adds to the definition of game derived from GA 1831, s 2 two bird species and one animal species namely woodcock, snipe and rabbits as well as the birds and hares defined by that section).

The section reads:

> if any person whatsoever shall commit any trespass by entering or being in the daytime upon any land in search or pursuit of game, or woodcocks, snipes, or conies,[11] such person shall, on conviction thereof before a justice of the peace, forfeit and pay such sum of money, not exceeding level 3 on the standard scale,[12] as to the justice shall seem meet.

The daytime is statutorily defined by virtue of GA 1831, s 34 as beginning at the start of the last hour before sunrise and concluding on the expiry of the first hour after sunset. The section refers to 'being in the daytime upon any land in search or pursuit of game'. Search is thus one of the two alternative prerequisites of the offence together with pursuit. If the Justices are not convinced to the criminal standard of the defendant's intention to search, then the case should be dismissed.[13] It is not necessary to secure a conviction to show that either the searching or the pursuing were with the intention or killing or taking at the time or of taking the bird into the defendant's possession.[14] It is clear that the game has to be alive at the time the pursuit or searching for begins. It is interesting to note the difference between this offence and the offences created under the Hunting Act 2004 (HA 2004).

The section creates another offence which is committed by five or more persons trespassing. This should be read with the offence committed by five or more persons under GA 1831, s 32:

> ... if any persons to the number of five or more together shall commit any trespass, by entering or being in the daytime upon any land in search or pursuit of game, or woodcocks, snipes, ... or conies, each of such persons shall, on conviction thereof before a justice of the peace, forfeit and pay such sum of money, not exceeding level 4 on the standard scale as to the said justice shall seem meet.

---

[11]   Ie rabbits.

[12]   As noted below, if only one Justice were to hear the case the maximum fine that could be imposed is £1, see Magistrates Courts Act 1980, s 121.

[13]   See *Dyer v Park* (1874) 38 JP 294.

[14]   See *Tiff v Billington* (1901) 65 JP 424.

The section provides for some defences to both offences created by it. These defences include that the alleged trespasser or trespassers had permission or the legal right to be there, in other words that he or they was or were not trespassing. As can be seen from the text of the statute quoted below, the wording of the section also prevents occupiers giving permission to third parties to enter land to kill or take game unless they have it themselves. The defences also deem the lord of the manor to be the legal occupier of the waste land of his manor and common land in his manor even though, as now, the likelihood in most parts of England and Wales is that he or she will not be.

The subsection containing the statutory defences reads:[15]

> Provided always, that any person charged with any such trespass shall be at liberty to prove, by way of defence,

> any matter which would have been a defence to an action at law for such trespass; save and except that the leave and licence of the occupier of the land so trespassed upon shall not be a sufficient defence in any case where the landlord, lessor, or other person shall have the right of killing the game upon such land by virtue of any reservation or otherwise, as herein-before mentioned;

> but such landlord, lessor, or other person shall, for the purpose of prosecuting for each of the two offences herein last before mentioned, be deemed to be the legal occupier of such land, whenever the actual occupier thereof shall have given such leave or licence;

> and that the lord or steward of the crown of any manor, lordship, or royalty, or reputed manor, lordship, or royalty, shall be deemed to be the legal occupier of the land of the wastes or commons within such manor, lordship, or royalty, or reputed manor, lordship, or royalty.

3.14   Game Act 1831, s 31

Section 31 empowers the person who holds the game rights over a parcel of land or their gamekeeper to require trespassers in pursuit of game to leave the land on penalty of them committing a criminal offence and for them to detain that person pending the alleged offender being taken to appear before the local magistrate. The powers under s 31 given to

---

[15]   The text of the section is extremely terse so it has been broken down into its component parts to make it more readily understood.

gamekeepers are also given coextensively to police constables by virtue of GA 1831, s 31A, which was inserted by the Police and Criminal Evidence Act 1984.[16]

This part of the section reads:

> Where any person shall be found on any land in the day-time,[17] in search or pursuit of game, or woodcocks, snipes, or conies, it shall be lawful for any person having the right of killing the game upon such land, by virtue of any reservation or otherwise, as herein-before mentioned, or for the occupier of the land (whether there shall or shall not be any such right by reservation or otherwise), or for any gamekeeper or servant of either of them, or for any person authorized by either of them, to require the person so found forthwith to quit the land whereon he shall be so found, and also to tell his christian name, surname, and place of abode; and in case such person shall, after being so required, offend by refusing to tell his real name or place of abode, or by giving such a general description of his place of abode as shall be illusory for the purpose of discovery, or by wilfully continuing or returning upon the land, it shall be lawful for the party so requiring as aforesaid, and also for any person acting by his order and in his aid, to apprehend such offender, and to convey him or cause him to be conveyed as soon as conveniently may be before a justice of the peace; and such offender (whether so apprehended or not), upon being convicted of any such offence before a justice of the peace, shall forfeit and pay such sum of money, not exceeding level 1 on the standard scale, as to the convicting justice shall seem meet.

The persons entitled under this section to require a name and address are thus wider than the owner of the right to kill or take game but also include occupiers (presumably legal occupiers rather than trespassers) and gamekeeper together with 'servants' for which read in modern parlance employees. The offence under this part of the section can also be committed not only by refusing to give a name and address or answering the question as to name and address vaguely but also refusing to leave the land or returning onto the land (presumably after promising to leave).

---

[16]   It is not necessary for a trespasser to both quit the holding and give his name and address, one will do before he can be apprehended, see *R v Prestney* (1849) 3 Cox CC 505, which seems to overrule *R v Long* (1836) 7 C&P 314, which held that both needed to have been done before apprehension was permitted.

[17]   See GA 1831, s 34 for a definition of daytime.

It is punishable with up to a level 1 fine on the standard scale unless only one Justice were to hear the case as the section envisages, in which case the fine cannot exceed £1.[18] The section provides for the offender to be detained only for up to 12 hours and if not brought before the magistrate by then to be released. This part of the section would not apply if the arrest was using police powers. The subsection reads:

> Provided always, that no person so apprehended shall, on any pretence whatsoever, be detained for a longer period than twelve hours from the time of his apprehension until he shall be brought before some justice of the peace; and that if he cannot, on account of the absence or distance of the residence of any such justice of the peace, or owing to any other reasonable cause, be brought before a justice of the peace within such twelve hours as aforesaid, then the person so apprehended shall be discharged, but may nevertheless be proceeded against for his offence by summons or warrant, according to the provisions herein-after mentioned, as if no such apprehension had taken place.

It is in the writer's opinion unlikely that in the 21st century it is realistic for a citizen to detain an alleged criminal for as much as 12 hours; it is likely that in reality the police would be called and thus this section is probably redundant.

3.15   Game Act 1831, s 32

Section 32 also creates a further offence which arises where five or more persons are found on land in search or pursuit of game, woodcock, snipe or rabbit (note again the extended class of species covered by the section beyond the definition of game derived from GA 1831, s 2). The penalty is a fine not exceeding level 4 on the standard scale. This part of the section reads:[19]

> Where any persons, to the number of five or more together,
>
> shall be found on any land, in the daytime,
>
> in search or pursuit of game, or woodcocks, snipes, or conies,
>
> any of such persons being then and there armed with a gun,
>
> and such persons or any of them shall then and there, by violence, intimidation, or menace, prevent or endeavour to prevent any persons authorized as herein-before mentioned from approaching such persons so found, or any of them, for the purpose of requiring them or any of them to quit the land whereon they shall be so found,

---

[18]   See Magistrates Courts Act 1980, s 121.

[19]   Again, to make it easier to understand the section has been broken up.

or to tell their or his own Christian name, surname, or place of abode respectively, as herein-before mentioned,

every person so offending by such violence, intimidation, or menace as aforesaid,

and every person then and there aiding or abetting such offender,

shall, upon being convicted thereof before two justices of the peace, forfeit and pay for every such offence such penalty, not exceeding level 5 on the standard scale, as to the convicting justices shall seem meet which said penalty shall be in addition to and independent of any other penalty to which any such person may be liable for any other offence against this Act.

Note again the wider class of species protected and that the offence can only be committed in the daytime; night offences are caught by the poaching legislation. Note also the requirement for the offenders to be armed and for them to use 'violence intimidation or menace'. The class of persons entitled to ask for a name and address is the same as the preceding section. Given the ingredient of the offence, it would be a brave landowner or gamekeeper who would approach such a body of persons, which limits the modern utility of this offence.

The powers vested in a police constable under GA 1831, s 31A coextensively with a gamekeeper have been buttressed by GLAA 1960, s 2. A police constable who has reasonable grounds for suspecting that an offence is being committed on any land under GA 1831, s 30 or under several sections of the NPA 1828[20] may enter onto land to exercise his s 31A powers or make an arrest under Police and Criminal Evidence Act 1984, s 25.

Land for this purpose includes Crown land, Duchy of Lancaster, Duchy of Cornwall land and land belonging to a government department but not various lands in government ownership specified in s 2(3).

By virtue of GLAA 1960, s 4, a police constable:

by or in whose presence he was apprehended may search him [ie the alleged offender] and may seize and detain any game[21] or rabbits, or any gun, part of a gun or cartridges or other ammunition, or any nets, traps, snares or other devices of a kind used for the killing or taking of game or rabbits, which are found in his possession.

---

[20]   See Chapter 7.

[21]   The definition of 'game' in the Poaching Prevention Act 1828 and the GA 1831 is the same save that bustards appear to still be included in the former statute.

This power is without prejudice to any other power the constable may have to search a suspect and detain chattels. Under GLAA 1960, s 5(2) a court may also order the confiscation and or destruction of game, rabbits or equipment in the convicted person possession.

If a person is convicted under that part of GA 1831, s 30 which deals with being one of five persons involved in the commission of an offence, and a vehicle was involved in the offence, the forfeiture provisions set out in GLAA 1960, s 4A may be invoked. This section is thus designed to deal with organised poaching gangs using vehicles to assist them to commit crime (as is likely in a rural location). This section only applies to the GA 1831 offence and therefore is dealt with in this chapter in more detail that the other sections where consideration here would duplicate the examination of the section in the context of poaching in Chapter 7. The section was inserted into the GLAA 1960 by Criminal Justice and Public Order Act 1994, s 168(1).

The section allows forfeiture of a vehicle in a convicted person's possession or belonging to him at the relevant time which has been used for the purpose of committing or facilitating the offence without regard to any restriction on forfeiture in any enactment.[22] Facilitating the commission of the offence includes the commission of certain acts after the offence has been committed. A court may later order that the owner of the vehicle may claim it back it if he is not the person from whom it was forfeited and can satisfy the conditions under the section provided the application is made within 6 months of forfeiture.

The above is a brief summary of the section which is best considered by reference to the actual verbatim text of the statute in full as it constitutes a self-contained code for all aspects of vehicle forfeiture arising out of a GA 1831, s 30 or a poaching conviction. It reads as follows:

(1) Where a person is convicted of an offence under section thirty of the Game Act 1831 as one of five or more persons liable under that section and the court is satisfied that any vehicle belonging to him or in his possession or under his control at the relevant time has been used for the purpose of committing or facilitating the commission of the offence, the court may make an order for forfeiture under this subsection in respect of that vehicle.

(2) The court may make an order under subsection (1) above whether or not it also deals with the offender in respect of the offence in any other way and without regard to any restriction on forfeiture in any enactment.

---

[22] Query if this section would survive a challenge under European Convention on Human Rights, Art 6 (fair trial procedure) or Art 1, First Protocol (right to property)?

(3) Facilitating the commission of the offence shall be taken for the purposes of subsection (1) above to include the taking of any steps after it has been committed for the purpose of:

(a) avoiding apprehension or detection; or

(b) removing from the land any person or property connected with the offence.

(4) An order under subsection (1) above shall operate to deprive the offender of his rights, if any, in the vehicle to which it relates, and the vehicle shall (if not already in their possession) be taken into the possession of the police.

(5) Where any vehicle has been forfeited under subsection (1) above, a magistrates' court may, on application by a claimant of the vehicle, other than the offender from whom it was forfeited under subsection (1) above, make an order for delivery of the vehicle to the applicant if it appears to the court that he is the owner of the vehicle.

(6) No application shall be made under subsection (5) above by any claimant of the vehicle after the expiration of six months from the date on which an order in respect of the vehicle was made under subsection (1) above.

(7) No such application shall succeed unless the claimant satisfies the court either that he had not consented to the offender having possession of the vehicle or that he did not know, and had no reason to suspect, that the vehicle was likely to be used for a purpose mentioned in subsection (1) above.

(8) An order under subsection (5) above shall not affect the right of any person to take, within the period of six months from the date of an order under subsection (5) above, proceedings for the recovery of the vehicle from the person in possession of it in pursuance of the order, but on the expiration of that period the right shall cease.

(9) The Secretary of State may make regulations[23] for the disposal of vehicles, and for the application of the proceeds of sale of vehicles, forfeited under subsection (1) above where no application by a claimant of the property under subsection (5) above has been made within the period specified in subsection (6) above or no such application has succeeded.

(10) The regulations may also provide for the investment of money and the audit of accounts.

(11) The power to make regulations under subsection (9) above shall be exercisable by statutory instrument which shall be subject to annulment in pursuance of a resolution of either House of Parliament.

(12) In this section, 'relevant time', in relation to a person convicted of an offence such as is mentioned in subsection (1) above, means the time when the vehicle was used for the purpose of committing or facilitating the commission of the offence, or the time of the issue of a summons in respect of the offence.

---

[23] No regulations appear to have been made to date under this section.

Whilst there are regular reports in the shooting press of these powers being used, the writer is not aware of any cases reaching the appellate courts as yet. Prosecutors are not afraid where a poacher is caught with cash proceeds to use the Proceeds of Crime Act 2002 to confiscate the money as well as to seek an order under GLAA 1960, s 4A in relation to the vehicle.

3.16 Game Act 1831, ss 30 to 32 – case law

In contrast to the paucity of cases in relation to other parts of the GA 1831, ss 30 to 32 of the Act have given rise to much litigation, much of it with inconsistent outcomes in terms of defining what the sections mean and how they are applied in practice. The sections were often used historically by aggrieved landowners to found actions in the criminal courts against neighbours or their staff presumably in pursuit of a wider dispute. It will be seen that in order to be guilty of the offence or trespass in pursuit of game the courts have tried to develop principles linking the killing of the game to the entry onto the land of another in what the writer refers to in the analysis of the cases that follows as the 'all one continuous act' analysis. Some cases have been discussed in the course of setting out the wording of the statute if the point made is brief. Here it is necessary to set out the text of the cases somewhat more fully and so a more detailed treatment is required.

In *Osbond v Meadows*,[24] Mr Meadows was on his own land (or land on which he had the right of shooting) when he fired and killed a pheasant on the adjoining land of the employer of the complainant James Osbond who was a gamekeeper. Meadows then went onto that land and picked it up. The court held that to commit an offence under GA 1831, s 30 the shooting and the entry had to be one continuous act. Erle CJ giving the leading judgment of the court stated:

> ... I am satisfied to give my judgment for the appellant, on the ground that, in substance and reality, the shooting of the bird and going upon the land to pick it up was one transaction. The respondent being on the land of an adjoining owner fires at a bird and kills it, and he immediately steps upon the land to pick up the dead bird. The act of going on the land to pick up the bird relates to the act of shooting, and the whole was one transaction.

This principle has not been consistently applied. In *Kenyon v Hart*,[25] a prosecution was brought under GA 1831, s 30. At first instance the appellant had indicated on oath that he was the under keeper to Sir

---

[24] (1862) 142 ER 1044.

[25] (1865) 6 Best and Smith 249, and 122 ER 1188.

Richard Tufton Bt and had seen the respondent out shooting. He alleged the respondent had shot a cock pheasant and it fell on a field occupied by a Mr Tappenden, the field being owned by Sir Richard Tufton. He went and fetched the bird himself taking his dog and gun with him. The respondent was on his own land when he shot the pheasant and it rose off his land. The pheasant was dead when the respondent picked it up and it lay on its back. The defence which was run by the respondent was that no trespass had been committed as the pheasant rose off the respondent's land and he was on his own land when he shot the bird. Giving a unanimous judgment of the court, Blackburn J stated:

> in *Osbond v Meadows* the justices drew the conclusion the whole was part of the same transaction ... it is enough that the question they ask us not about the pheasant having been hit whilst it was in the air over the neighbour's land but whether the entry on the land to pick up the dead pheasant was a trespass within this statute. It was a trespass but not in pursuit of game and we cannot as in *Osbond v Matthews* infer that it was all one act.

An example of a stern judge setting high standard of disproof for a defendant is *Burrows v Gillngham*[26] where a gunshot was heard emanating from a wood and a man ran out with a gun and three dogs; the man admitted shooting a pigeon but nothing more. The court held that these facts were admissible evidence of the commission of an offence under GA 1831, s 30.

It is very difficult to draw any firm principle from these cases as to how the 'all one continuous act' analysis for committing this offence is likely to be applied. The interpretation by the judiciary in the 19th century seems to have been very subjective and there are regrettably no modern cases to provide a more up-to-date view on how this issue would be interpreted now.

The 'all one continuous act' analysis is developed further in the next case we need to consider. In *Tanton v Jervis*,[27] Mr Tanton one of a party shooting pheasants saw pheasants that had been shot fall into the wood of Mr Henry Simmons. Two days afterwards Mr Tanton went into Mr Simmons' wood to pick up the pheasants believing them to be dead and was summonsed under GA 1831, s 30 for trespassing in pursuit of game. Giving the judgment of the court, Field J said:

> I think it is clearly established that if this pheasant had been dead when the appellant went into the wood to pick it up this would not be searching for game within the meantime of Section 30 of The Game Act.

---

[26]   (1893) 57 JP 432.

[27]   (1879) 43 JP 784.

This was despite the fact that he held that the appellant committed a trespass but he held that the trespass was not in pursuit of game because it was dead. He also explored in his judgment in some detail the requirement for the game to be live at the time it was pursued in order that an offence is committed.

This case can be contrasted with the case of *Horn v Raine*[28] where a man standing on his own land shot into the land of another person and killed a grouse. He did not go onto the land to pick it up but went away returning some hours afterwards. Lord Russell of Killowen CJ in giving the leading judgment to the court, stated:

> the facts in this case are simple enough. The respondent standing on his own land fired a shot over the wall into the land of another person and killed a grouse sitting there. He did not follow that up immediately or do anything more at that moment but some hours afterwards he went onto the land where he had killed the grouse and went and entered upon the land. Under such circumstances and satisfied unrestricted he went there in search of what he had killed. In my opinion that is sufficient to connect the two things together and it seems to me that in so entering upon the land to search for an pick up the bird he was committing an offence specified in Section 30 of the Act.

He then continued:

> I ought to add that in the state of facts as proved it seems to me that it did not matter in the least whether the game was living or dead when he went in search of it.

The case law cannot be relied upon to found definite principles as to what constitutes the ingredients of the offence. Certainly, however, the sooner that one pursues game on another's land shot on or over that land the more likely one is to be convicted but it would appear that even if one waits this still can be one continuous act. Shooting a bird on or over one's own land would not appear to be a good defence if it lands on the land of another as, although one thereby owns the carcase, the criminal offence is all about trespass in pursuit and not legal ownership.

There are some esoteric points on the law of trespass in pursuit of game. *Pochin v Smith*[29] is authority for the proposition that where a party is the tenant of a parcel of land and the landlord of that land has not reserved the game rights back to himself and the tenant then grants the lease to a third party to get in and cut the hay, the third party has authority to grant the shooting rights to a fourth party who cannot then be liable under GA 1831, s 30 for trespassing in pursuit of game.

---

[28]   (1898) 62 JP 420.

[29]   (1887) 52 JP 4.

The law of highways is somewhat complex but the case of *R v Pratt*[30] is authority for the proposition that one can commit the offence of trespassing in pursuit of game on a public road. In this case the land under the running surface of a highway was in the ownership of the party on whose land the trespass was alleged to have taken place. The trespasser sent his dog onto the land next to the road without entering personally onto it, a pheasant flew up and he shot at it whilst on the road. The road was held to be in the occupation of the land owner. The rationale for this being that he was not on the roadway in exercise of his right of way but for another purpose, namely in search of game and was thus a trespasser. It was held that the sending of the dog into cover though a trespass would not amount to a conviction because the statute required a personal entry by a human rather than by his dog.

3.17   Shooting over water

There are no specific rules applying to shooting over tidal waters which differentiate the position between shooting over land constituting tidal waters (ie the foreshore) and shooting over land such that GA 1831, ss 30 to 32 might be applied in a different way. Non-tidal waters are treated in law as if they were land. In the case of the foreshore, a shooting lease needs to be obtained from the Crown if the area in question is in Crown ownership. An explanation as to how to do this is set out on the Crown Estate website.[31]

3.18   Exemption for hunting

The terms of s 35 have been greatly altered by the HA 2004. Prior to the amendment they provided in effect a defence for any person hunting or coursing upon land with hounds and being in pursuit of deer, hare or fox from being found to be trespassers in pursuit of game within the meanings of ss 30 to 32 and 36.[32] The section now, as amended by the HA 2004, reads as follows:

---

[30]   (1855) 4 E&B 860.

[31]   www.crownestate.co.uk.

[32]   For a modern case dealing with civil trespass and hunting and examining the law in detail, see *League Against Cruel Sports Ltd v Scott and others* [1986] QB 240.

> Provided always, that the aforesaid provisions against trespassers and persons found on any land shall not extend to any lord or any steward of the crown of any manor, lordship, or royalty, or reputed manor, lordship, or royalty, nor to any gamekeeper lawfully appointed by such lord or steward within the limits of such manor, lordship, or royalty, or reputed manor, lordship, or royalty.

and thus provides no defence to persons who might be hunting perfectly legally within one of the exemptions to the HA 2004 to a prosecution under the GA 1831 for trespassing in pursuit of game.[33] It is difficult to see what purpose this section now serves as in most cases the categories of persons protected would have the right to enter on lands within the manor in any event. Is it really intended to allow the lord of the manor and his servants to be allowed to enter onto lands in his manor even if the sporting rights are elsewhere, ie with a sporting or farming tenant? A literal reading of the section can only lead to that conclusion. There appears to be no case law as yet where this section has been considered.

Formerly prior to amendment by the HA 2004 the words: 'to any person hunting or coursing upon any lands with hounds or greyhounds, and being in fresh pursuit of any deer, hare, or fox already started upon any other land, nor' were contained in the middle of the text, which in effect validated any trespass in pursuit of deer hares or foxes.

3.19   Confiscation of illegally taken game

Section 36 allows a person having the right of taking the game on the land or any gamekeeper or servant or for the occupier of the land (whether or not the right of sporting has been reserved to him) either by day or by night to demand the game from that person and to seize and take it from him if not handed across.

To use such powers now would be likely to attract the opprobrium of the police and, given the sorts of persons engaged in poaching, lead to a breach of the peace and be very dangerous. For this reason the section is practically redundant.

---

[33]   Assuming that they are pursing game; foxes or deer are not game, see GA 1831, s 2.

3.20   Time limit for prosecutions

For completeness it is appropriate to mention s 41, which provides that every prosecution for offences punishable by summary conviction under the Act (which are all of them) shall be commenced within 3 calendar months after the commission of the offence.

3.21   Prosecutions and civil trespass actions

Section 46 specifically preserves the ability of an aggrieved landowner to raise a civil action for trespass but provides that when somebody has been prosecuted under the terms of the GA 1831 no civil action at law will lie for the same trespass, ie the double jeopardy is eliminated. The Act states:

> Provided always, that nothing in this Act contained shall prevent any person from proceeding by way of civil action to recover damages in respect of any trespass upon his land, whether committed in pursuit of game or otherwise, save and except that where any proceedings shall have been instituted under the provisions of this Act against any person for or in respect of any trespass, no action at law shall be maintainable for the same trespass by any person at whose instance or with whose concurrence or assent such proceedings shall have been instituted, but that such proceedings shall in such case be a bar to any such action.

Note that it is explicit from the terms of the statute that right to bring a civil action for trespass is lost if the proceedings in the criminal court are begun even if they are not successful. It is not known what 'concurrence and assent' means in a scenario when an independent prosecutor brings criminal proceedings without the agreement of a complaint but it is submitted in practical terms given the modern practice of the Crown Prosecution Service that this is unlikely.

3.22   Summary

- In summary, therefore, the GA 1831 is a statute which was revolutionary in its time and the effect of which has been hugely modified by the RRO 2007.

- There are four areas of control still left governed by the GA 1831 which are explained at para 3.3.

- Sections 3, 3A and 24 are still of some use in determining the times of the year and of the day and week when birds might be taken, but in the long run do need to be subsumed into the WCA 1981 to give the same powers of enforcement in relation to game species as in relation to other wild birds.

- The terms of ss 7 to 12 are candidly obsolete by virtue of changes in property law since 1831 such that either in a landlord and tenant or freehold around grantee of a profit situation the rights will be dealt with in any event.

- The sections in relation to gamekeepers are so archaic and obsolete as to be almost worthy of repeal without further ado.

- The several criminal offences created by GA 1831, ss 30 to 32 are worthy of retention, but in the long run should be consolidated into a new statute which should also sweep up the various poaching prevention acts and offences created by the WCA 1981.

4 The Right to Sport or to Kill or Take Game

4.1 Introduction

The rights to hunt, shoot and sport together with other associated rights, for example the rights to rear, preserve or keep game (which for concision in the examples below are referred to as 'the rights') exist, it is submitted in the following possible combinations and or ways:

(1) The freeholder holds the land and the rights with no third party involvement; this situation is not considered in this chapter, which focuses on the conflicts over the usage of the rights which potentially arise when one person holds the rights and the other occupies the land.

(2) The rights are held by a freeholder and the tenant holds and occupies the land with no rights.

(3) The rights and the land are held by the tenant. The landlord will hold anything outside the terms of the grant and thus its drafting as is the case with all such conveyancing will be very important.

(4) The freeholder holds no rights, they being leased to a third party often called a shooting tenant and the land is let to a farming or rural landowning tenant

(5) The land is owned by a freeholder but the rights are reserved out of the freehold to a former owner or third party who holds the sporting or shooting rights.

It is of course principally scenarios (2), (4) and (5) in which disputes and thus case law arise. Whilst there is a potential for disputes in scenario (3), it is seldom that a case proceeds to court over the drafting of such a reservation. In relation to situations where the farmer (for want of another term, ie the party not holding the rights who occupies the land) disagrees with the methods used to exploit the use of the rights by another these concerns have been to an extent ameliorated by the existence since 1880 of the inalienable right to shoot rabbits and hares; so called ground game. As further explained in Chapter 5, before this date much distress was caused to farming tenants in particular by the reservation to their landlords of the right to shoot rabbits and hares leaving them unable to control rabbit numbers and causing wholesale losses of revenue.

In Chapter 2, which considers the definition of 'game', we examined some cases in which disputes had arisen as to what the words of the grant in each case allowed the holder of the rights to do and what species were allowed to be taken. The chapter centred on the definition of game used in each of the particular cases. That discussion it is submitted sits best with the chapter dealing with the definition of game but needs now to be revisited in this chapter. This is because in defining the nature of rights the same issues are visited in defining what the grant permits to be hunted or shot as much as the species and how the shooting and hunting is to be carried out. Each case contains an example of a court considering particular drafting and coming to a particular conclusion. The purpose of this chapter is to examine the meaning of the terms 'game rights' or 'sporting rights' whether in a freehold or leasehold framework together with terms used in association with them, for example the right to rear and preserve game and to consider some propositions that arise about such rights. It also looks at some specific issues which arise in connection with leasehold grant of sporting or shooting rights.

As can be seen from Chapter 2, the term 'game rights' has no real meaning except that which it is defined to mean in the document that creates the rights. The term 'sporting rights' it is thought connotes a wider meaning than game rights and includes the ability to take all creatures in common parlance considered to be the subject of sport.[1]

4.2   The legal nature of a sporting or shooting right

Whether in a freehold or leasehold context the right to take game or to sport is in its nature a *profit à prendre*, ie it is a right to enter another person's land, to shoot or to sport and to take something (in this case a wild creature reduced into one's possession once dead) from it. As such, a profit is an incorporeal hereditament.[2] It has long been held (see *Wickham v Hawker*[3] for example) that the right to hawk hunt and fowl is a *profit à prendre*.

---

[1]   See *Jeffryes v Evans* (1865) 19 CBNS 246.

[2]   An examination of the scheme of the Law of Property Act 1925 and the scheme of legal estates and interests that it created is beyond this work, suffice it to say that s 2(a) designates an incorporeal hereditament as a legal interest.

[3]   [1835–42] All ER Rep 1.

In *Wickham v Hawker* when giving the judgment of the court, Parke B stated:

> ... it appears to us that the liberties to Hawk Hunt Fish and Fowl granted to one, his Heirs and assigns, are interests or profits á prendre may be exercised by servants in the absence of the master. Further we think that the addition 'with servants or otherwise' does not limit the privilege and exclude the exercise of it by servants.

It is submitted that the right to shoot or kill species of wild birds is analogous to this and is also such a *profit*. This view is supported by the Court of Appeal in *Pole v Peake*.[4] *Pole v Peake* is an important case giving rise to several legal propositions relating to game reservations and is examined in detail at para 4.6.

Profits à prendre unlike easements can exist in two forms: first, in gross, ie attached to a person and burdening a particular area of land and, second, appurtenant profits which attach to a parcel of land known as a dominant tenement and burden another area known as the servient tenement. Both forms can be created and transferred as we have seen by deed. In addition if not created by deed they may be established as having arisen by prescription (ie long use) both at common law and under the Prescription Act 1832 and under the doctrine of Lost Modern Grant. They may arise as with easements by a sale of part implying a grant under Law of Property Act 1925 (LPA 1925), s 62. The period of exercise for the Prescription Act 1832 requirements to be met are respectively 30 years or 60 years (replacing the periods of 20 years and 40 years as would apply in the case of easements). The period for establishing Lost Modern grant is still however 20 years.[5] It is not thought that a right in the nature of a *profit à prendre* in gross has been established by prescription in modern times.

Appurtenant rights have been registerable at HM Land Registry for as long as land has been registerable for the area in question. Rights in gross have only, however, been registerable since 13 October 2003 as a result of changes made by the Land Registration Act 2002. Readers who need to know more on this subject will be assisted by the excellent HMLR Practice Guide 16.[6]

---

[4] (1998) *The Times*, 22 July 1998, also reported at [1998] EGCS 125.

[5] See *Lord Dynevor v Richardson* [1995] 1 All ER 109.

[6] Available at www.hmlr.gov.uk/temppages/practice.htm.

In practice, the problems that are most often encountered in a field sports context with respect to a particular *profit à prendre* are not how it arose but instead focus on the nature and quality of the grant which has been made. Unless stated in express terms, a *profit* is not an exclusive grant nor is it limited so that one might have a right to shoot which is shared with the owner of the dominant tenement and both are unlimited. The maintenance of the land burdened by the right is also in practice an issue. In practice, a problem which often arises is the land falling into poor repair.

4.3   Transmission of sporting and shooting rights

Generally speaking (because there are notable exceptions) *profits à prendre* can only be transmitted from one owner to another by deed. LPA 1925, s 52(1) reads:

> All conveyances of land or of any interest therein are void for the purpose of conveying or creating a legal estate unless made by deed.

Incorporeal hereditaments are caught by LPA 1925, s 52, by virtue of the definition of land contained in s 205(ix), which defines land as:

> (ix) 'Land' includes land of any tenure, and mines and minerals, whether or not held apart from the surface, buildings or parts of buildings (whether the division is horizontal, vertical or made in any other way) and other corporeal hereditaments; also a manor, an advowson, and a rent and other incorporeal hereditaments, and an easement, right, privilege, or benefit in, over, or derived from land (emphasis applied by underlining).

A notable exception to the rule that transfers of such rights have to be by deed is derived from LPA 1925, ss 52(2)(d) and 54(2)[7] which exempt parol (ie leases not created by deed) leases of 3 years or shorter from a requirement to be by deed. Likewise, Law of Property (Miscellaneous Provisions) Act 1989, s 2(5) exempts short leases from having to be in writing. A tenancy of an agricultural holding which is from year to year, for example under the Agricultural Holdings Act 1986 (AHA 1986) need not be by deed and its terms as to the shooting or sporting rights would be binding although the document was not a deed.

---

[7]   Which exempts the requirement for oral short leases to be in writing and thus be a conveyance. This reads 'leases taking effect in possession for a term not exceeding three years (whether or not the lessee is given power to extend the term) at the best rent which can be reasonably obtained without taking a fine'.

There are cases, particularly those reported before the reforms of land law and conveyancing in 1925, where the document creating the right was not by deed and where this fact was used in attempt to get out of the arrangement previously entered into usually without success.[8] It would generally not now be a defence that would find favour as the court would apply the doctrine of *Walsh v Lonsdale*[9] to make the so called agreement a contract to create a lease. It is beyond the scope of this work but the courts have also generally been ingenious in getting round defences based on a failure to comply with Law of Property (Miscellaneous Provisions) Act 1989, s 2[10] (formally LPA 1925, s 40).[11]

It follows that as a *profit à prendre* is an interest in land, not only can it be enforced by parties to the original agreement but also its rights and obligations can be enforced by successors in title. For example in *Hooper v Clarke*,[12] a landowner granted an exclusive right of licence to take game on his land with the use of the cottage to the defendant. In return, the defendant covenanted to leave the land at the end of the term as well stocked with game as at the time of the original grant of the lease. The reversion in the land was subsequently transferred to the claimants who then bought an action at the end of the term for breach of covenant alleging that the requisite game had not been left as required by the grant. The court had no difficulty in finding that this being a *profit à prendre* it ran with the land and as such the claimant was entitled to sue upon it.

4.4 Legal nature and effect of a reservation of shooting

In situations where a freeholder has kept back the rights to shoot, hunt or sport from the sale of the land to another freeholder or has let the land to a farmer or other tenant, the reservation takes effect as a re-grant by the party to whom the freehold is transferred or who takes the benefit of the lease as tenant.

---

[8] See for example *Bird v Higginson* [1835–42] All ER Rep 171, and *Adams v Clutterbuck* (1882) LR 10 QBD 403.

[9] (1882) 21 Ch D 9. Based on the equitable maxim that 'Equity treats that as done which ought to be done'.

[10] Which requires contracts to sell interests in land to be in writing and signed by both parties.

[11] Cases such as *Tomlinson v Day* [1821] 2 Brod & Bing 680, and *Webber v Lee* (1818–82) LR 9 QBD 315 are, it is submitted, likely to be decided differently or at least more easily under the modern law if argued now.

[12] (1867) LR 2 QB 200.

The House of Lords confirmed as much in *Mason v Clarke*[13] where Viscount Simonds in his judgment stated:

> it is clear law that the so called reservation operates as a re-grant of the rights therein described in favour of the landlord and his assigns and is such a *profit á prendre* is created.

Later cases have expressed some dissatisfaction with this doctrine but have not demurred from it. In *Pole v Peake*,[14] which is considered at length at para 4.6, Buxton LJ stated in his judgment:

> it was agreed that, under the admittedly anomalous rule recognised by this Court in *Johnstone v Holdway* [1963] 1 Q.B. 601, [1963] 1 All ER 432 and the St Edmondsbury case (*St Edmondsbury and Ipswich Diocesan Board of finance v Clarke (number 2)* [1975] 1 All ER 772, [1975] WLR 408) these 'reservations' operated law as re-grants by the purchaser in a fee simple, who is in respect of them subject to the principles of contra proferentem and inability to derogate from his grant.

It will be seen therefore that the practical consequence of a reservation taking effect in law as a re-grant is to provide that if there is any ambiguity in the wording of a grant its construction should be against the party who imposed it into the contract. The result of following this fiction is that this will not be the party reserving the right back to himself but instead the party who has to bear the burden of it. This is also anomalous because of course the documentation would generally have been drafted by and to favour the seller.

4.5   Damage caused by the sporting tenant to the freehold in defence of his rights

Once possessed of the right to shoot, hunt or sport, the question arises as to what extent the holder of those rights is entitled to do damage to the landlord's or freeholder's land or property in pursuance of the defence of the rights when he takes steps to protect them which damages the freehold. To what extent should he be held to account? The cases seem to show the answer to that question is that he has to do quite a lot to be held responsible for damage caused to the freeholder's land and is given a margin of appreciation by the courts in defending and asserting his rights.

---

13   [1955] AC 778 (a case principally about ground game rights).

14   (1988) *The Times*, 22 July 1998, also reported at [1998] EGCS 125.

An example of this is the case of *Cope v Sharpe (No 2)*[15] where the claimant who was the landowner let the shooting rights to a sporting tenant. A heather fire broke out on part of the claimant's land. The defendant, who was the head keeper of the sporting tenant, with a view to protecting the defendant's property set fire to patches of heather between the main fire and a covert in which the defendant's pheasants were preserved in order that the main fire, when it reached the bare patches left when the fire had burned out, would have nothing to feed on and would just die out – he was, in effect, creating a fire break. The case, which was tried by a jury, resulted in a finding that although the creation of the firebreak turned out to be unnecessary, the defendant reasonably believed that it was necessary and was entitled to succeed in his defence. In short, his actions were reasonably necessary to defend the right which had been granted to his employer.

Each case where a sporting tenant takes action to defend sporting rights will, it is submitted, turn on its own facts as to whether or not acts by the sporting tenant to protect his rights will be objectively justifiable. The situation where the landowner does acts which are likely to damage the sporting tenant's rights is considered at para 4.9.

4.6   Pole v Peake[16]

Pole v Peak is authority for at least four propositions relating to the construction of game reservations in a freehold context, three of which are considered below and one in the next paragraph. It was a relatively modern (1998) case where the law in relation to reservations by the freehold owner was considered at length by the Court of Appeal, and which assists greatly in explaining how a reservation were it to be litigated now is likely to be construed by the appellate courts.

The defendants in this case were the freeholders of a smallholding in Devon in respect of which the sporting rights had been reserved to the claimants. The claimants had in fact leased off the sporting rights to a syndicate. The defendants challenged the manner and method of use in which the sporting rights were being used. The claimants sued for damages alleging that the defendants' farming activities amounted to interference with their rights. The defence maintained by the defendants was that no damage had been suffered by the claimants and the defendants counterclaimed seeking to establish that the claimants'

---

[15]   [1912] 1 KB 496.

[16]   (1998) *The Times*, 22 July 1998, also reported at [1998] EGCS 125.

sporting rights were restricted by standards of reasonableness and that their rights should be balanced against the right to farm so that the faming was not unduly affected. This became known in the appellate judgment as the '*balance of rights arguments*'.

The judge (a recorder at first instance) declined to grant the claimants an award of damages but was prepared to grant a series of declarations (mostly in favour of the claimants) which were then challenged by the defendant appellants when the matter came before the Court of Appeal. The principal part of the reservation which was litigated and featured most heavily in the analysis in the judgments (and by far the shortest part of the drafting considered by the court) was reservation '(b)' which read:

> the exclusive rights with or without friends servants and others to hunt shoot fish and sport over and upon all or any part of the lands woods premises hereby conveyed and to kill and take and dispose of all game rabbits wild fowl and other animals wild animals and birds and fish upon the said lands woods and premises and for any of the purposes aforesaid and also for the purpose of preserving and rearing game wild fowl and fish to enter upon the said lands woods and premises or any part thereof.

It should be noted that this was quite a sophisticated grant – it was not merely a bare right to shoot or hunt – in that it allowed access for various purposes including for rearing and preserving game.

The first proposition we can derive from this case arises because the recorder found at first instance that the word 'game' in the deed included pheasants reared for the purposes of sport irrespective of whether they bred naturally on the estate and/or they were originally wild. This finding was upheld by the Court of Appeal.

The second proposition concerns the rights of access in favour of the sporting right owners. Buxton LJ also considered (and was supported by the other members of the Court of Appeal in his finding) that no prior notice was required to be given by the owners of the sporting rights, their servants or agents before they exercised rights of access.

His judgment states:

> entry is permitted not only for sporting but also for the purposes of preserving game, an activity that was agreed to extend to eradicating predators, for instance by shooting foxes. It can scarcely have been intended that a keeper seeing a fox on the appellants land is obliged to give prior notice before entering to dispose of it.

The third proposition from this case relates to at what time (ie is it at trial or the date of grant) that one judges the actual condition of the holding and thus use of the rights. The argument run in this case by the defendants was that the use to which the rights could be put was that use at the time of the grant of the deed giving rise to the rights in 1974 and not the larger and more extensive right used at the time of trial. Buxton LJ said in respect of that argument:

> the case of the profit such as the present seems to me to be *a fortiori* of the case of an easement that was addressed in *White v Grand Hotel Eastbourne Limited* [1913] 1 Ch 113. If the use that may be made of a right of way to a specific property is not to be cut down by a reference to the use of that property at the time of the grant that must also be the case with a profit, unless that limitation is specified in the grant which here it is not.

Much later in the judgment he would turn to this issue again when he said:

> ... I was not persuaded by the argument which by the end of the appeal may not have been persisted in that activity on the property should be judged by its condition at the date of the deed, when it was, on various views of the evidence other scrubland or rough grazing land. The conveyance to the appellants envisaged the land's use for farming as demonstrated by the terms of part (a) of the reservation and it would in my view be inconsistent with the terms of that grant and for the appellants to be held down to the use of the land in the condition that it was in 1974.

The fourth proposition concerns excessive stocking of the holding with birds which, as it fits neatly in with the subject of the next paragraph, is considered below.

As has been seen just about everything that might be argued about between parties on either side of a dispute about sporting rights was argued about in *Pole v Peake*. It is in the writer's opinion essential reading not only for practitioners who argue about such rights but also those who draft them. Although now over 35 years old (24 years old at the time of the case) the drafting in this case stood up well to examination and practically allowed the sporting right owner to do just about what they liked, including acts in building up number of birds which otherwise would have been in law an actionable nuisance.

4.7   Excessive stocking of shoots

On the subject of excessive numbers of birds being allowed to accumulate on the land but then damaging interests of the farmer, the state of the law may be illustrated by examining three apparently inconsistent cases.

In *Farrer v Nelson*[17] (a case often cited in game cases) the facts were that the defendants held the sporting rights, the claimant was the farmer. It

---

[17]   (1885) 15 QBD 258 (Divisional Court).

was demonstrated during the trial that the defendants had, during the spring, summer and autumn of 1884, reared in coops elsewhere than on the claimant's farm but on another part of the estate about 1500 pheasants and had carried in the coops about 450 of these pheasants to a coppice wood situated on the claimant's farm but reserved to the landlord in the claimant's lease. About an acre of the coppice wood had been cut down for the purposes of rearing pheasants into which the 450 pheasants were brought. Part of the coppice wood adjoined within about 5 yards of the fence dividing the coppice wood from the claimant's field in which the damage which the claimant complained of was being done. As many as 100 pheasants at a time had been seen running in the claimant's field adjoining the coppice in the month of August when the grain and other crops were ripening. The field in which the damage was done covered an area of about 27 acres and the coppice wood in which the pheasants were placed covered together about 80 acres.

Giving the judgment of the court, Pollock B said:

> I will first deal with the question of when an action can be brought by a neighbour against any person who collects animals on his land so as to injure the crops of the neighbour and I should say beyond doubt such an action would lie …

This seems to say that just getting together what is objectively too many birds on a parcel of land is actionable but it is not as simple as that; somewhat anomalously he then went on to say:

> as I understand the law each person in this country is entitled to bring on his land any quantity of game which can reasonably and properly be kept on it and so that nothing extraordinary and non-natural is done. The case of *Birkbeck v Paget*[18] which was cited by the Counsel for the Defendants to show that there is a difference between introducing fresh game and shifting game from one part of the land to the other is in any rate an authority that the lessee is not warranted in introducing into the land game not breed in the ordinary way. So here so long as the lessee of the right of shooting was exercising the ordinary rights which the landlord who had reserved the right might have exercised he was acting within his rights but the moment he brings on game for an unreasonable amount or causes it to increase to an unreasonable extent he is doing that which is unlawful and action may be maintained for his neighbour for the damage which he has sustained.

It is submitted that what the judgment in this case tells us is that the starting proposition when considering an action based on allegation of excessive game stocking is that one is entitled to stock land with as many birds as one likes given that they are wild but that once they amount in

---

18   [1862] 31 Beav 403.

law to a non-natural user (presumably analogous with the use of the same words in *Rylands v Fletcher*[19]) the use becomes actionable. A better description in the writer's view is that what is meant in modern analysis is an actionable nuisance.

This proposition may be contrasted and refined by the findings of the Court of Appeal in *Pole v Peake*.[20] In the *Pole* case, protection was clearly afforded to the owner of the rights against an action for nuisance by the wide and express terms of the grant. We must therefore look first at the use and the excessiveness of the use and then look at what the words of the grant permits as the latter may excuse what, in the absence of the latter, would be a nuisance and thus actionable.

When the Court of Appeal in *Pole* considered the subject of building up the numbers of birds on the holding such that the farming operations were damaged, the case was clearly decided in favour of the holder of the shooting rights. As has been stated in summary, the wide terms of the drafting of the document were such that the document effectively validated what would otherwise have been at law a nuisance.

Buxton LJ stated:

> ... I have held, the respondents who are entitled under the grant to bring birds on to the property even if those birds interfere with or damage the farming operations, they cannot be liable if such interference or damage is caused by birds straying from elsewhere.

As can be seen, the court's decision principally in relation to the preserving and rearing part of the drafting might conceivably have been different had those words not been included and the right had been limited to sporting only. It is important therefore when drafting a document to consider precisely what one wishes to do and to reserve appropriate rights back to one's self. Otherwise if the rights are challenged the contemplated rights may not actually be achievable in practice.

A contrary finding but one which reflects the analysis based on non-natural user above is to be found in what is admittedly a first instance decision of Romer J in the case of *Seligman v Docker*,[21] the case incidentally being decided in 1948 and in game law terms being relatively modern. In this case the defendant owned shooting rights over some 4,230 acres of which 2,326 acres were let to the claimant. Ninety percent of the

---

[19]   (1868) LR 1 EX 265.

[20]   (1998) *The Times*, 22 July 1998, also reported at [1998] EGCS 125.

[21]   [1949] Ch 53.

pheasant shooting was on two of the farms within the estate. During the shooting season in 1947 to 1948 the defendant's coverts were filled with an inordinate number of wild pheasants which, in their search for food, gravely damaged the claimant's crops. The claimant sought an injunction which would have barred the defendant from bringing onto any land occupied by the defendant an unreasonable quantity of pheasants or allowing them to collect or encouraging them to collect. The judge held that the presence of the large number of pheasants on the defendant's coverts was not due to any unreasonable action by the defendant within the meaning of the words used in *Peech v Best* by Scrutton LJ[22] (see also the analysis of this case below) but was due to the exceptional weather conditions prevailing in the summer of 1947 particularly in May and June, and that the defendant was not under a legal obligation to the claimant to reduce or disburse the pheasants when it became known that the number was so considerable given that they were *ferae naturae*. Other factors pointing to this conclusion were the fact that the claimant had no right to shoot them and the law did not impose any duty on the defendant to shoot them himself.

The decision, therefore, whether or not the accumulation on a parcel of land A of an unreasonable number of pheasants damaging part of land B will depend upon the circumstances in which the birds gather, whether the use is unreasonable and or constitutes a legal nuisance and the respective drafting of the rights and obligations of the owners of A and B themselves. There can be no definitive answer as to whether or not the accumulation of a large number of pheasants or indeed any other game species causing damage to a farming operation is in itself actionable, but these cases do give some guidance on judicial attitudes albeit not very current attitudes.

Thus far we have examined circumstances in which disputes have arisen about the number of birds which could be accommodated on the particular parcel of land and the use to which the sporting tenant or owner of the sporting rights could put the land.

4.8   Turning out game not bred on the holding

We have considered the issue of excessive stocking and formulated some principles for how the court might approach this issue, but what about bringing birds not bred on the holding onto the holding to increase the

---

[22]   '.. both Landlord and sporting tenant must use their land reasonably with regard to the interest of the other and will be liable for damage caused to the other by extraordinary non natural or unreasonable action'.

number to be shot there? In *Pole v Peake* we saw that the grant expressly permitted this, but what if it does not and all that is reserved is a right to shoot?

The case of *Birkbeck v Paget*[23] is authority for the proposition that the exclusive right of shooting being leased to a sporting tenant over a farm does not justify the shooting tenant in turning out on game not bred there in the ordinary way and justifies the landlord in keeping down the excess. This should be contrasted with the previous case law on overstocking and illustrates neatly the points made.

Conversely, it was found in *Bird v Great Eastern Railway Company*[24] that when a person takes on a right of shooting or fishing he takes on the game or fish as may be there and there is no contract on the part of the person letting the right that he will keep up the quantity of game or fish in the absence of an express contractual obligation which was not in that case present (see the judgment of Erle CJ). This case arose in circumstances where the owners of land agreed to let a house and some land and the sole right of shooting and fishing over other land. The defendant railway company purchased part of the land on which the landowner had agreed to let the right of shooting, the railway was constructed on it and the shooting on the part which was not purchased was diminished in value. The claimant claimed compensation from the railway company. This is not in itself inconsistent with the previous cases, the principal issue to consider it is submitted is what does the grant require and/or permit?

4.9   Freeholder endangering rights of the sporting tenant

We must now address the situation where the owner of the sporting rights considers that the freeholder or an outside agency on his behalf is endangering those rights and takes steps to protect them. To what extent should the freeholder be held to account in changing the use of part of the holding which affects the shooting or sporting rights? The cases seem to show that he does not have to do much to show that he has infringed those rights and thus be required to pay damages, but an injunction is a different matter.

---

[23]   (1862) 31 Beav 403.

[24]   (1865) 19 CBNS 268.

In *Pattisson v Gilford*[25] the owner of an estate, the shooting over which had been let, issued sale particulars seeking to sell the estate in 13 lots. The particulars said that the estate contained several plots of accommodation and building land suitable for the erection of villas and residences and describing one lot in particular as well situated for the erection of a house. The particulars showed that it was intended to construct a road through the estate and dedicate the road to the public but it did say that the estate was subject to rights of shooting. The sporting tenant issued proceedings seeking an injunction preventing the development and/or the sale and the case came on for hearing at an interlocutory stage. Giving the judgment of the court, Sir George Jessell MR said:

> it does not by any means follow that of necessity the erection of one or two villas will injure the right of shooting; that depends upon the part of the estate on which the villas are built, the number of villas and the size and so on. There may or may not be injury and I should hesitate long before I grant an injunction against the Defendant over those whose estate there existed a right of shooting to prevent building a single house.

He also then went on to say:

> I know nothing of preventing a landlord who is granted the right of shooting over his estate from after selling his estate in lots. He may have 50 lots or 500 lots. It might be very inconvenient for the owner of the right of shooting if he had to sue a great many parties and bring about many actions; I still take it his right of shooting does not necessarily interfere with the division of the estate in lots.

In order to do some justice he did however order an enquiry as to damages, and *Pattisson v Gilford* must be seen against a background of an application to the court in some ways too soon before the true damage which was done to the sporting rights might be defined. The claimant here would almost certainly get damages but not the injunction he sought because damages were almost certainly an adequate remedy.

In *Gearns v Baker*,[26] the landlord granted shooting rights over 1300 acres to the claimant and proposed to cut down some of the coverts on the land and sell the timber. The Court of Appeal refused in the facts of this case to restrain an infringement of the grant of shooting rights. James LJ stating:

> it is preposterous to suppose that a man who grants a shooting lease for 21 years is to be dictated to by this Court as to whether he should cut down a tree or remove a coppice, because by so doing he would be driving away the hares or interfering with the breading of the pheasants. If men need to acquire such rights they must express their meaning clearly. I believe that

---

25   (1874) LR 18 Eq 259.

26   [1874–75] LR 10 Ch App 355.

such rights are not expressed and not implied in the ordinary grant of shooting, and that this right has no right to interfere in the way suggested. As this case stands it is the common case of a man who is granted a right of shooting and is minded to deal with his estate as other land owners deal with their estates, and I am at the opinion that there is no right of power in this court to interfere with him in so dealing.

An example of a case following this judicial approach of being loathe to grant an injunction if only a small part of the shoot is interfered with (in that the claimant got his damages but no injunction) is *Peech v Best and others*,[27] where the facts were that the owner of a farm containing 700 acres granted to a grantee for a term of 14 years *'the exclusive right of shooting and sporting in an over'* the farm. Whilst the lease had some 4 years to run the grantor sold 12 acres which consisted of part of the 700 acres to a purchaser who to the knowledge of the grantor intended to use this portion as training stables for race horses. Immediately after the sale but before the conveyance the purchaser employed a builder who began to clear the land conveyed and to erect the house for the purchaser and enough for six stable boys and 31 loose boxes. The court in this case considered *Pattisson v Gilford* (and indeed *Gearns v Baker* considered above) but the lengthy judgments of several judges is best summarised by the judgment of Sleesser LJ who stated:

> in the present case the learned judge having heard the evidence has come to the conclusion that the Plaintiff has suffered damage from the physical obstruction of sporting rights. He has not found, nor indeed was it seriously suggested that the use of the land for racing stables was in any way reasonably necessary or at all connected with the farm management. I think this is a case where the injury done cannot be said to fall within the principle of *Gearns v Baker* and that what was done was not for the management of the land rather the case resembles *Dick v Norton* where the timber was felled solely for mercantile purposes in which case damages were given by an experienced Chancery Judge. It was said that the learned Judge should have considered only what had been done which is the erection of the buildings. The learned Judge here has apparently confined the damage to the injury already done but I read him to have given them in lieu of the injunction claimed for breach of covenant and in that case damages can be given in respect of the injury which would have been prevented by the injunction if granted ... I think this appeal must be dismissed.

The final case to consider on this area is *Well Barn Shoot Limited and others v Shackleton and others*.[28] In this case the claimant company sold a farm on its estate to the defendants, reserving the sporting rights back to itself. The

---

[27]   [1931] 1 KB 1, CA.

[28]   [2003] EWCA Civ 2.

defendants then applied for planning permission to convert two barns into residential units. The company issued proceedings alleging that this development would interfere with its sporting rights. The court applied the principles in *Peech v Best* as to whether or not there would be a substantial interference with the rights of the sporting tenant. They however distinguished this case from *Peech v Best* where the landowner owned all of the land and had granted the sporting rights over the whole of the estates and where the question to be considered in *Peach v Best* was whether or not building on 12 acres amounted to an interference with those rights. The defendants in *Well Barn Shoot Limited* had only granted back to the claimants the rights over their farm land.

The judge at first instance approached the matter applying the decision of Scrutton LG in *Peech v Best*:

> it appears to me that fundamentally changing the character of the land over which the sporting rights are granted ... if it has the necessary effect of substantially enduring the rights of others is a derogation from grant, and the substantive interference with the *profit à prendre* granted.

The judge at first instance indicated that the other two activities which were relevant to that issue were, first, the passage on foot twice a week during the shooting season for the purpose of driving birds over the guns and, second, the recovery of shot birds which may have fallen back into the farmyard and lands. Ultimately, he ended up granting declarations which were held to be reasonable by the Court of Appeal. It is submitted that the decision might very well have been different had access been needed to the farmland in question for the purposes of guns standing on the land to shoot rather than the limited rights to access for beating and for recovering birds.

4.10   Agricultural holdings and game damage[29]

For completeness, it is best here to include an explanation of what is objectively an anomalous statutory intervention in relation to leasehold sporting grants or reservations which affects how the terms of a grant and the common law would otherwise treat the issue of game damage.

Farming tenants whose tenancies are protected by the AHA 1986 and who suffer the situation where their farming activities are disrupted by game crop damage can, subject to satisfying the conditions set out in

---

[29]   For a more extensive examination of this area of the law see *Scammell and Densham's Law of Agricultural Holdings* (LexisNexis, 9th edn, 2007), especially para 24.11.

AHA 1986, s 20, recover compensation for their losses. Under the terms of AHA 1986, s 20(4), the extent of any damage is to be decided by arbitration. Such arbitration would now be conducted under the Arbitration Act 1996. As with all matters touching and concerning the Act, contracting out of the s 20 procedure is prohibited by AHA 1986, s 78(1) and is likely also to be prevented even if that might be got round for policy reasons arising out of the House of Lords' approach to this issue in *Johnson v Morton*.[30]

Section 20(1) reads:

> Where the tenant of an agricultural holding[31] has sustained damage to his crops from any wild animals or birds the right to kill and take which is vested in the landlord or anyone (other than the tenant himself) claiming under the landlord, being animals or birds which the tenant has not permission in writing to kill, he shall, if he complies with the requirements of subsection (2) below, be entitled to compensation from his landlord for the damage.

Note that compensation is claimable not just for damage suffered from normally recognised game or sporting species but 'any wild animal or bird'. The wording allows claims against the landlord not only for damage caused by the landlord but also where the landlord has let off the reserved sporting or shooting rights to his sporting tenant. The situation where the tenant has let the right back to the landlord would also be caught by the wording of s 20(1). The wording was narrower before the passing of the AHA 1986 and previously limited compensation to damage from game species, but this approach was abandoned in the Agricultural Holdings Act 1984, the predecessor to the AHA 1986. Likewise, compensation in previous statutes was limited but is now subject to proof unlimited.

The requirements in s 20(2) are:

> (2) ... the tenant shall give his landlord—
>
>> (a) notice in writing within one month after the tenant first became, or ought reasonably to have become, aware of the occurrence of the damage,
>>
>> (b) a reasonable opportunity to inspect the damage—
>>
>>> (i) in the case of damage to a growing crop, before the crop is begun to be reaped, raised or consumed, and
>>>
>>> (ii) in the case of damage to a crop which has been reaped or raised, before the crop is begun to be removed from the land, and

---

[30]   [1980] AC 37, HL.

[31]   For a definition of 'agricultural holding', see AHA 1986, ss 1(1) and (6).

(c) notice in writing of the claim, together with particulars of it, within one month after the expiry of the year in respect of which the claim is made.

The terms of s 2 should be read in conjunction with s 2(3) which reads:

(3) For the purposes of subsection (2) above—

(a) seed once sown shall be treated as a growing crop whether or not it has germinated, and

(b) 'year' means any period of twelve months ending, in any year, with 29th September or with such other date as may by agreement between the landlord and tenant be substituted for that date.

Unlike the notice of claim which has to be in writing, the agreement to adopt a different date for the shooting year to run can be made verbally but is of course best recorded in writing.

The landlord who has let off his sporting and shooting rights is protected by s 20(5) which reads:

(5) Where the right to kill and take the wild animals or birds that did the damage is vested in some person other than the landlord, the landlord shall be entitled to be indemnified by that other person against all claims for compensation under this section; and any question arising under this subsection shall be determined by arbitration under this Act.

As mentioned before an arbitration under that Act is now an arbitration under the Arbitration Act 1996. He can thus recover any award against him from his sporting or shooting tenants.

If the landlord does not pay after an arbitration award is made the tenant can obtain a charging order over the freehold by virtue of AHA 1986, s 85(2).

In the writer's experience, the problem in using this section is proving that the source of the damage is the landlord's fault. Ground game often cause much damage and it is a brave expert who can identify the damage caused by rabbits as opposed to the damage caused by other species on the same holding. In addition, most standard reservations do not include deer in the species reserved to the landlord, which cause as much damage as any species whilst no compensation would be claimable under s 20 unless the right to sport, shoot or take deer were reserved to the landlord.[32]

---

[32] Whether compensation might be claimed at common law for eg nuisance is a different matter.

4.11   Tenancies under the Agricultural Tenancies Act 1995

There is no equivalent to AHA 1986, s 20 in the Agricultural Tenancies Act 1995 (ATA 1995) which makes no mention of the issue at all. In accordance with the Act's policy of freedom of contract the arrangements will have to be negotiated or the tenant will be left with a common law claim for nuisance, the strength of which will depend as reported above on the precise terms of the landlord's reservation.

None of the standard farm business tenancy precedents in the *Encyclopaedia of Forms and Precedents*[33] or indeed any other precedent books the writer has considered make express provision for game damage without a bespoke clause being inserted during the course of drafting.

4.12   Shooting rights over water and the foreshore

If for no reason other than the fact that wild fowling is an activity carried out by a significant number of people involved in shooting it is important to explain the special rules that apply in relation to shooting over water.

The right to shoot will depend upon whether or not one is shooting over tidal or non-tidal waters. Non-tidal waters including rivers and lakes are treated just the same as any other land. The issue will be whether or not the grant of shooting covers the area in question. The issue of the boundary between adjoining lands is usually decided by the Latin maxim *usque ad medium filum*,[34] in other words one looks at the centre line of the river or lake and this is the boundary. This is only a presumption and therefore the boundary may be in a different position either by previous agreement or otherwise.

The position in relation to the foreshore (being defined as the area between mean high and mean low water marks) is different from non-tidal waters. The Crown Estate owns virtually the entire seabed to the 12 mile nautical territorial limit. In relation to the foreshore, the Crown owns approximately 55% of this. The Crown also owns approximately half of the beds of estuaries and tidal rivers in the United Kingdom. In all other cases the rights of ownership will have vested by either a grant or on some other basis in a private individual. There is no right vested in

---

[33]   The Rt Hon Lord Millett and Robert Walker (eds) (LexisNexis, 2010).

[34]   Always to the middle.

the public to shoot or otherwise take game and other non-game birds and animals over the foreshore. It is possible to apply for licences from the Crown managing agents to shoot. It is also possible by shooting for a sufficient period to acquire a prescriptive right by long use.[35]

4.13   Summary

It can be seen from the extensive consideration of the cases above that the case law by no means makes it easy for the student of game law when considering what a particular word, phrase or reservation means, or how the law responds in a particular situation. It can be seen from the analysis above how fact-specific each case is and how the wording effects the decision one way or the other time and time again. There are, however, some themes to judicial thinking which it is hoped have been brought out in the analysis. It is submitted, however, that the following propositions can be distilled from the cases:

- A right of sporting or shooting is a *profit à prendre* or right analogous to it and will run with the land and be enforceable by subsequent land owners.

- As such, it can only be transferred at law by deed.

- This requirement does not apply to short (less than 3 years) or verbal leases.

- The law will usually assist situations of informal agreements which ought to have been by deed or in writing to do justice.

- A reservation in a deed operates in law as a grant to the seller and is to be construed against the purchaser who is also deemed to be the party who drafted it in case of ambiguity (*contra proferentem*).

- The owner of the sporting right can take reasonable steps to preserve that right, including acts which would otherwise be a trespass.

- A right to shoot does not in the absence of express additional words imply the right to bring game onto land or rear game on the land.

- Up to a point a landowner who has granted away the sporting or shooting rights can use his land as he wishes, but there are uses mainly of a non-agricultural nature which will infringe the rights and give rise to a claim for an injunction or damages.

- The courts are usually loathe to grant injunctions in such cases.

---

[35]   The Crown Estate website is most helpful in this area, www.thecrownestate.co.uk.

- Merely advertising for sale or lotting up the property will not amount to such a situation.

- An action can lie for overstocking a holding with game.

- Whether a shooting tenant can be sued for overstocking his land with game depends upon the wording of the grant. A grant to merely shoot or sport will afford no protection, whereas a more extensive grant allowing rearing or preserving game will protect from what otherwise would be a nuisance.

- There is no obligation to keep a particular amount of game on a holding implied on either landlord or sporting tenant in the absence of express words.

- The right to shoot includes the right to take game away.

- The right to preserve game includes the right to kill and keep down pests and vermin.

- Rearing game includes bringing birds onto the holding for that purpose.

- The activity on a holding at the date of a claim is not generally to be judged by the activity at the time of grant of a right unless expressly stated in the words of the grant.

- The definition of game in deed will generally include birds brought onto the holding and not just those naturally occurring on the holding in the absence of specific words to the contrary.

- There is help provided in the AHA 1986 in the case of tenants not only for game damage but damage from all wild animals in certain circumstances.

- This provision has not been replicated in the ATA 1995, so specific provision needs to be made in the tenancy agreement for compensation provisions.

5   Ground Game

5.1   Introduction

Ground game is defined as rabbits and/or hares[1] and is a relatively new concept to game law arising by statute and unknown before the statute was passed. The Ground Game Acts, being the GGA 1880 as amended by the Ground Game (Amendment) Act 1906, constituted when enacted a revolutionary change in favour of farming tenants over the previously existing law. Prior to enactment, landlords habitually reserved the right of shooting rabbits and hares to themselves and then did nothing to prevent crop damage from those species, leading to justifiable feelings of dissatisfaction on behalf of farming tenants, particularly when they were prosecuted when using self-help remedies in seeking to cull what were seen by them as vermin.

It is easiest to illustrate the policy of the GGA 1880 by examining and then commenting on each operative section of the Act. It should be noted before doing so that by virtue of GGA 1880, s 9, a person acting in accordance with the GGA 1880:

> shall not thereby be subject to any proceedings or penalties in pursuance of any law or statute.

In addition GGA 1880, s 10 makes it clear that:

> Nothing in this Act shall authorise the killing or taking of ground game on any days or seasons, or by any methods, prohibited by any Act of Parliament in force at the time of the passing of this Act.

This shows the clear parliamentary intent to make this statute paramount in achieving its aim of allowing the control of ground game by occupiers of rural land.

GGA 1880, s 1 creates, subject to conditions, a right vested in the occupier of land[2] to kill ground game concurrently with the holder of the right to do so either in the lease of the land or otherwise (eg if those rights have been reserved out of the freehold to another as a *profit à prendre*. The first part of the section reads:

---

[1]   See GGA 1880, s 8.

[2]   Note the statute does not refer to tenants or licences just occupiers.

> Every occupier of land shall have, as incident to and inseparable from his occupation of the land, the right to kill and take ground game thereon, concurrently with any other person who may be entitled to kill and take ground game on the same land ...

The Act does not define the term 'occupier'. It is submitted that after all the litigation on the subject of property rights after the passing of this statute, an occupier could conceivably now be either a freeholder (or now a commonholder), a leaseholder,[3] a licensee or a trespasser. Does the Act intend all of these to have the right to shoot ground game? There is no guidance in the Occupiers Liability Acts 1957 and 1984. Occupier there being defined, first, by what duty a person owes and, second, by reference to the 1957 statute as being a person who owes the duty under s 2 of the 1957 Act. Although one might at first blush take the view therefore that giving the word its widest meaning would tend to such a construction and despite there being no authority on the point, the writer's view is that a court would go some way to prevent a trespasser from being legally able to take ground game relying on this Act. Whilst we cannot define precisely who is an occupier we can define who is not. As can be seen later in this chapter, two classes of persons are deemed not to be occupiers.

The section then goes on in s 1(1) to provide three provisos to the general principle derived from the first part of the section. These are, to quote that section verbatim:

> (1) The occupier shall kill and take ground game only by himself or by persons duly authorised by him in writing:
>
> (a) The occupier himself and one other person authorised in writing by such occupier shall be the only persons entitled under this Act to kill ground game with firearms;
>
> (b) No person shall be authorised by the occupier to kill or take ground game, except members of his household resident on the land in his occupation, persons in his ordinary service on such land, and any one other person bona fide employed by him for reward in the taking and destruction of ground game;
>
> (c) Every person so authorised by the occupier, on demand by any person having a concurrent right to take and kill the ground game on the land or any person authorised by him in writing to make such demand, shall produce to the person so demanding the document by which he is authorised, and in default he shall not be deemed to be an authorised person.

---

[3] Which might range from a tenant at will through to a tenant with lease of many thousands of years.

A suggested form of written appointment of a person to kill ground game using a firearms is set out at Appendix A1.

Section 1(b) provides that no person shall be authorised by the occupier to kill or take ground game except certain classes of persons including persons in his ordinary service. The case of *Savile v Yateman*[4] (which concerned whether or not the testator had left a legacy to certain of his servants) contained an examination of the difference between indoor and outdoor servants but is not particularly illuminating here because the statute presumably is meant to include persons working on the land itself rather than indoor domestic servants. *Ogle v Morgan*[5] applied the proposition that the gift by will of persons is 'a servant in a domestic establishment at the time of my decease' does not include a head gardener. It is also arguable that farm workers working on cottages rented from a farm owner might on a wide construction of this term be held to be members of the household. The cases seem to show that residents is a case of fact for the judge to determine in each case and that relatively short period of residence, perhaps as little as a week, can be construed as being sufficient for the purposes of the Act. The Act's terms are, however, insufficient to unequivocally show that a contracting company that uses a considerable number of persons for the purposes of clearing rabbits from rabbit-infested land is wholly within the law.

A further proviso is created by s 1(2) in that holders of right of common or holders of short leases do not qualify as occupiers:

> A person shall not be deemed to be an occupier of land for the purposes of this Act by reason of his having a right of common over such lands; or by reason of an occupation for the purpose of grazing or pasturage of sheep, cattle, or horses for not more than nine months.

Section 1(3) deals with moorland and as it describes unenclosed land not being arable lands. In modern parlance this is mountain moor and health land. This section needs to be read with Ground Game (Amendment) Act 1906, ss 2 and 3. The sections will be set out one after another and discussed:

> 1(3) In the case of moorlands, and uninclosed lands (not being arable lands), the occupier and the persons authorised by him shall exercise the rights conferred by this section only from the eleventh day of December in one year until the thirty-first day of March in the next year, both inclusive; but this provision shall not apply to detached portions of moorlands or uninclosed lands adjoining arable lands, where such detached portions of moorlands or uninclosed lands are less than twenty-five acres in extent.

---

[4]   (1887) 576 LT 475.

[5]   (1852) 1 De GM&G 359.

2   Notwithstanding anything in section one, subsection (3), of the Ground Game Act, 1880, contained, the occupier of lands to which that subsection applies shall, without prejudice to his existing rights under that Act, be entitled, between the first day of September and the tenth day of December, both inclusive, in any and every year, to exercise the right of killing and taking ground game by the said Act conferred otherwise than by the use of firearms.

3   Section three of the Ground Game Act, 1880, shall not apply to prevent the occupier of lands to which section one, subsection (3), of that Act applies, and the owner of such lands or other persons having a right to take and kill game thereon from making and enforcing agreements for the joint exercise, or the exercise for their joint benefit, of the right to kill and take ground game between the first day of September and the tenth day of December, both inclusive, in any or every year.

As can be seen, the terms of GGA 1880, s 1(3) establishes a close season for the killing of ground game from 11 December to 31 March (unless the lands are as described as detached or less than 25 acres) but the Ground Game (Amendment) Act 1906 extends this period to include the period 1 September to 10 December but limits its utility in reality by preventing the use of firearms in that period.

The Ground Game (Amendment) Act 1906 allows cooperation between occupier and the holder of the right to take ground game from 1 September to 10 December. Firearms are not mentioned but of course the prohibition on firearms will only apply to the extent that the terms of the GGA 1880 is solely being relied upon and not where a wider contractual or other right is being exploited.

5.2   Anti-avoidance

GGA 1880, ss 2 and 3 need to be read together and provide the mechanism by which the Act provides for the occupier always to be able to kill ground game whatever the legal paperwork says. It is convenient to deal with the two sections together. Section 2 reads:

Where the occupier of land is entitled otherwise than in pursuance of this Act to kill and take ground game thereon, if he shall give to any other person a title to kill and take such ground game, he shall nevertheless retain and have, as incident to and inseparable from such occupation, the same right to kill and take ground game as is declared by section one of this Act. Save as aforesaid, but subject as in section six hereafter mentioned, the occupier may exercise any other or more extensive right which he may possess in respect of ground game or other game, in the same manner and to the same extent as if this Act had not passed.

Section 3 reads:

> Every agreement, condition, or arrangement which purports to divest or alienate the right of the occupier as declared, given, and reserved to him by this Act, or which gives to such occupier any advantage in consideration of his forbearing to exercise such right, or imposes upon him any disadvantage in consequence of his exercising such right, shall be void.

Thus the occupier can give the right to kill ground game to another. Notwithstanding any purported agreement to give up a right to kill ground game, the occupier still keeps such a right if he does so. If he has a wider right vested in him by contract he can exercise it and if he tries to give up the right in any way the arrangement is void. This is subject a saving provision in s 5 which preserves contractual or leasehold arrangements in force at the time of passing of the Act[6] in favour of someone other than the occupier until such time as they shall determine. It is submitted that there are unlikely to be many if any arrangements still in force. The section also preserves:

> any special right of killing or taking ground game to which any person other than the landlord, lessor, or occupier may have become entitled before the passing of this Act by virtue of any franchise, charter, or Act of Parliament.

This would include for example such of the customary right vested in the lord of the manor *ratione privilegii* by virtue of ownership of the soil. The ancient right of franchise to kill or take game not incidental to the ownership of land was abolished by the Wild Creatures and Forest Law Act 1971.[7]

5.3   Night shooting, etc

Prior to its amendment by the WCA 1981, GGA 1881, s 6 prevented the killing of ground game at night. As originally passed, the first part of this section reads:

> No person having a right of killing ground game under this Act or otherwise shall use any firearms for the purpose of killing ground game between the expiration of the first hour after sunset and the commencement of the last hour before sunrise.

This section now needs to be read in conjunction with WCA 1981, s 12 (which declares that Sch 7 is to have effect) and WCA 1981, Sch 7, which reads:

---

[6]   In force from 7 September 1880.

[7]   See s 1(b).

(1) Notwithstanding the provisions of section 6 of the Ground Game Act 1880, it shall not be unlawful for the occupier of any land himself, or one other person authorised by him under section 1 of that Act, to use firearms for the purpose of killing ground game thereon between the expiration of the first hour after sunset and the commencement of the last hour before sunrise if (except where he has the exclusive right) the occupier has the written authority of the other person or one of the other persons entitled to kill and take the ground game on the land.

(2) In this paragraph 'ground game' means hares and rabbits.

As before, a written authority is needed if the occupier is not possessed of an exclusive right of killing ground game. The precedent at Appendix A1 is suitable for this purpose as well as for the purpose of satisfying GGA 1880, s 1(1).

5.4   Poison

The remainder of GGA 1880, s 6 prohibits the employment of poison for killing ground game in any circumstances.

5.5   Penalties for breach of Ground Game Act 1880, s 6

The penalty for those convicted of illegal night shooting or poisoning is in both cases a level 1 fine.

5.6   Right to bring proceedings

By virtue of s 7, a person who is not in occupation of land having the sole right to take game (note not just ground game) is given the same right to commence proceedings as an exclusive owner notwithstanding the rights of the occupier. The section is in reality a saving provision to prevent legal argument in future as to whether exclusive right of killing or taking game had been downgraded by this statute. The statute does not define game and it not necessarily to be defined as it is used in GA 1831, s 2. The section is somewhat opaque and reads:

> Where a person who is not in occupation of land has the sole right of killing game thereon (with the exception of such right of killing and taking ground game as is by this Act conferred on the occupier as incident to and inseparable from his occupation), such person shall, for the purpose of any Act authorising the institution of legal proceedings by the owner of an exclusive right to game, have the same authority to institute such proceedings as if he were such exclusive owner, without prejudice nevertheless to the right of the occupier conferred by this Act.

5.7 Ground Game Act 1880 – case law

In *Morgan v Jackson*,[8] the claimant was the occupier of a farm with the sole right of taking game and rabbits on it. He then agreed in writing to let the defendant for an annual sum '*the sole right of killing all winged game, hares and rabbits*' on the farm. When the parties fell out, the county court judge gave judgment for the defendant on the grounds that the agreement was void by virtue of GGA 1880, s 3 so far as it purported to give the defendant the sole right to kill hares and rabbits. The Court of Appeal held that the county court judge was wrong, Day J saying:

> in the present case the occupier had rights apart from the Act. He can within Section 2 be an occupier of land and entitled otherwise in pursuance of the Act to kill the ground game thereon. I can see nothing in Section 2 or Section 3 which prevents him from entering into a contract with another to allow that other to exercise the right which the occupier has.

In *Anderson v Vickery*,[9] the owner of a parcel of land granted to the claimant a lease of the sporting rights and then transferred the freehold to the defendant subject to the lease. The defendant entered into occupation of the land. When the parties fell out following the defendant starting to kill ground game, an action ensued and the Court of Appeal held by a majority that the defendant being an occupier was entitled to kill the ground game not under the terms of the Act but because he was the freehold owner.

In *Sherrard v Gascoigne*,[10] the claimants took a tenancy induced by a promise from the landlord's agent that if the claimant left the ground game unshot for the benefit of the defendant, the defendant would compensate him for the damage which would thereby be done to the claimant's crops by the ground game. When subsequently the claimant in breach of this agreement claimed compensation for the damage to the ground game, the Divisional Court held that the agreement was void and that he could do so. Darling J stating in the course of his judgment that:

> in my opinion it is perfectly clear that the agreement there alleged is an agreement which purports to alienate the right of the plaintiff to kill and take the ground game, which is given to him by the Act. It purports also to give the plaintiff an advantage in consideration of his forbearing to exercise his right within the meaning of Section 3. The agreement is therefore absolutely void and no claim under it can be enforced. The landlord has no right to kill and take the ground game unless by agreement.

---

[8] [1895] 1 QB 885, CA.

[9] [1900] 2 QB 287.

[10] [1900] 2 QB 279.

The provisions of *Sherrard v Gascoigne* illustrate an arrangement clearly in breach of the terms of the Act. *Stanton v Brown*,[11] however, is authority for the proposition that merely reserving the sporting rights does not breach the Act's terms and specifically s 3. In this case a lease was entered into for 7 years containing a reservation of the sporting rights. The lease then expired and continued orally. The tenant somewhat ingeniously then argued that the oral lease was different in the terms from the previous written lease. That point was decided against him in the course of the judgment. Channell J in the course of his judgment stated:

> looking at the provisions of Section 3 of the Ground Game Act 1880 it seems to me that the Section cannot mean that an agreement as to game which contains something in contravention of the occupier's right to destroy ground game is to be void in its entirety.

This was upheld as the unanimous view of the court such that where rights are reserved they are valid in their own terms provided the GGA 1880 rights inalienably reserved to the occupier are preserved.

Where authority has been granted to a third party other than the owner to kill game, that authority must be in writing.[12] The Scottish case of *Richardson v Maitland*[13] arose out of facts where Mr Richardson, a miner residing in a neighbouring village, was employed verbally at a salary of £2 per year by the tenant of the farm to shoot rabbits. The lease of the farm reserved the hares and rabbits to the landlord. Richardson had shot rabbits on the farm on the above footing for some 10 years when he was convicted of an offence contrary to the GA 1831. The High Court of Justiciary of Scotland held that as the lease reserved hares and rabbits to the landlord, that deprived the tenant of his common law right to kill rabbits and his only right was under the GGA 1880. That right he could not contract himself out of, but to give another a right to shoot rabbits under the statute requires the instruction should be in writing and there were no written authorities granted to Richardson here so that he was then guilty of the offence of trespassing in pursuit of game.

There are a number of cases dealing with the meaning of s 6 of the Act. *Leworthy v Rees*[14] is authority for the proposition that where an owner who occupies his own land sells to another person the right to kill or take rabbits on the land, such other person is not subject to the restrictions imposed by s 6 and may kill rabbits and hares at any time with or

---

[11]   [1900] 1 QB 671.

[12]   See GGA 1880, s 1(c).

[13]   (1879) 4 SLT 277.

[14]   (1913) 109 LT 244.

without firearms. A similar decision was reached in the case of *May v Waters*,[15] where the Act was held not to apply to a grantee of the right to kill and take ground game where the grantee was not the occupier of the land over which the right was granted.

In *Smith v Hunt*,[16] it was held that s 6 does not apply to an owner of land doing any of the acts prohibited on his own land. An attempt was made to expand the ratio of that case in *Saunders v Pitfield*[17] some 3 years later by trying to argue that an occupier with the right of shooting over the land does not come within this section. Smith J, giving the judgment of the court, stated in the course of his judgment:

> In *Smith v Hunt* we came to the conclusion that Section 6 did not apply to owners killing the ground game on their own land because it appeared to us that while the whole of the act was in derogation of the rights of owners, given the occupier's concurrent rights with them of killing the game, Section 6 was for their benefit to prevent the wholesale destruction of the ground game. It is now said that we must go further, and say, that because the rest of the Act is in favour of occupiers, Section 6 cannot be read as containing anything prejudicial to them, and that an occupier who has the right of shooting over his land does not come within the section, because if the Act had not been passed he would have a right to do the acts it prohibits. I do not think this is so.

Readers wanting a general examination of the issue of ground game of the House of Lords in a relatively modern case (which incidentally reversed the opinion of Denning LJ in the Court of Appeal) should see *Mason and another v Clarke*.[18] A company let a farm to a farmer and reserved to itself *'game, rabbits, wild fowl and fish with liberty for itself and other persons authorised by it to preserve, shoot, hunt, course, kill and carry away the same'*; the farmer agreed subject to the GGA 1880 not to shoot or otherwise sport on the land. In October 1950 the land owner prompted by a notice from the Ministry of Agriculture (due to rabbit infestation) orally agreed to let rabbiting rights to a rabbit catcher in the sum of £100. The rabbit catcher had extreme difficulty in carrying out his contract because of acts of interference by the tenant who specifically started removing snares, alleging they were interfering with his sheep which were grazing on the farm. Much of the judgment was involved in considering whether or not the receipt which had been provided was fraudulent and whether or not the original grant of the right to the rabbit catcher was valid because it was not under seal (although it was later confirmed as being

---

15   [1910] 1 KB 431.

16   (1885) 50 JP 279.

17   (1888) 58 LT 108.

18   [1955] AC 778, HL.

under seal by a subsequently entered into document). The Court held that the rabbit catcher was not aware of the alleged fraud and, therefore, was not debarred from enforcing an agreement that he had an enforceable right in equity to a *profit à prendre* having enjoyed sufficient possession of the farm, and that the acts of the farmer amounted to trespass on the real hereditament because he was the occupier of the land, and that laying snares in the circumstances was a perfectly proper exercise of rabbiting rights and not extraordinarily unreasonable and therefore would be allowed.

5.8   Summary

In summary the GGA 1880 provides as follows:

- Ground game means hares and rabbits.

- The GGA 1880 empowers occupiers to kill ground game whatever the terms of their tenancy.

- This right cannot be alienated even if the occupier wants to or tries to do so.

- The right is concurrent with the rights of the owner of the sporting rights.

- Only the occupier and one other are permitted to legally use firearms to kill ground game on a holding.

- The occupier can authorise his household, his servants and one person for reward to kill ground game on a holding subject to the point made in the previous bullet point.

- A written authority is required and a precedent of such an authority is to be found at Appendix A1.

- Holders of common rights or leases for a term of less than 9 months cannot be occupiers.

- Night shooting of ground game is now permitted but a written authority is again required. The precedent at Appendix A1 is also suitable for this purpose.

6 Closed Seasons

6.1 Introduction

The law prevents the taking of game and killing of game or other bird species in four ways. First, some species cannot be killed at any time, this being prevented by the WCA 1981 for example. These are often known as the Schedule 1 species. Second, the law allows the killing of some non-game species under general or specific licences issued under the WCA 1981. Third, some days of the year are proscribed for shooting and taking game, for example Christmas day and any Sunday.[1] Finally, the law regulates the time of year in which some game species and indeed non-game species can be taken, the former under the GA 1831 the latter under the WCA 1981. The WCA 1981 species are set out in Sch II to that Act. The scheme of this chapter is to consider those prohibitions in the order set out above and then to summarise the applicable law in the analysis at the end.

6.2 Prohibition on killing wild birds other than game birds under the Wildlife and Countryside Act 1981

The WCA 1981 consolidated and codified a large area of the law in relation to the protection of bird and plant species. It re-enacted and amended the Protection of Birds Acts 1954 to 1967 as well as empowering statutory regulation in a large number of areas relating to wildlife.

The scheme of the Act is to provide a statement of principle in s 1 and then to spend a large part of the Act qualifying that principle specifically in relation to game species.

Section 1(1) of the Act reads:

(1) Subject to the provisions of this Part, if any person intentionally or recklessly—

(a) kills, injures or takes any wild bird;

---

[1] See GA 1831, s 3.

(aa) takes, damages or destroys the nest of a wild bird included in Schedule ZA1;[2]

(b) takes, damages or destroys, destroys or otherwise interferes with the nest of any wild bird while that nest is in use or being built; or

   (ba) at any other time takes, damages, destroys or otherwise interferes with any nest habitually used by any wild bird included in Schedule A1;

   (bb) obstructs or prevents any wild bird from using its nest; or

(c) takes or destroys an egg of any wild bird, ...

On a first reading of s 1 without looking at s 27 (which contains the definition section of the WCA 1981) one might think that as all game species are wild birds (and indeed as one sees from Chapter 1 of this book they cannot be anything but wild birds) the killing or taking of them has been in some way prevented by the WCA 1981. Whilst WCA 1981, s 1 establishes a general principle that one should not kill or injure or take any wild bird, the law is that the killing or taking of game birds (including a much wider definition than that contained in GA 1831, s 2) subject to closed seasons is still permitted by the Act.

Wild bird is defined in s 27 of the Act, which sets out the definitions used in the Act as:

> any bird of a species which is ordinarily resident in or is a visitor to the European territory of any member state in a wild state but does not include poultry or, except in Sections 5 and 16, any game bird (or moor game) black (or heath) game or ptarmigan.

Section 1 carries on to deal with further offences of having in one's possession any live or dead wild bird or anything derived from such a bird or any egg of a wild bird or part of such an egg. A similar point can be made in relation to that offence in relation to game birds; there is of course already provision for the control of the taking of game bird eggs under GA 1831, s 24.

Defences are then set out in ss 3 and 3A and offences are created by subsection 5 in relation to nest building and the control of disturbance in relation to it.

WCA 1981, s 2 then quotes a list of exceptions to the general principle established by s 1 and is in the following terms:

---

[2]   Ie the golden eagle, white tailed eagle and osprey.

(1) Subject to the revisions of this section, a person shall not be guilty of an offence under Section 1 by reason of the killing or taking of a bird included in Part 1 of Schedule 2 outside the closed season for that bird, or the injuring of such a bird outside that season in the course of intending kill it.

There are now in fact no birds in Sch 2, Part 1. Schedule 1 lists a considerable number of species which are now fully protected, including somewhat interestingly the Gyr falcon which is not native to the United Kingdom.

Birds which are listed in Sch 2, Part 1 and which can be killed outside of the closed season include capercaillie, various species of duck and geese, golden plover, common snipe, teal, widgeon and woodcock.

Section 2(4) defines the closed season as:

(4) In this section and section 1 'close season' means—

(a) in the case of capercaillie and (except in Scotland) woodcock, the period in any year commencing with 1st February and ending with 30th September;

(b) in the case of snipe, the period in any year commencing with 1st February and ending with 11th August;

(c) in the case of wild duck and wild geese in or over any area below high-water mark of ordinary spring tides, the period in any year commencing with 21st February and ending with 31st August;

(d) in any other case, subject to the provisions of this Part, the period in any year commencing with 1st February and ending with 31st August.

Section 2(5) and 2(6) allow the Secretary of State to vary the closed season for any wild birds specified in the order or to provide extra protection for the birds by effectively putting them back into the cover provided by s 1 of the Act for a special protection period. Section 2(7) provides that before he can make an order under s 2(6), the Secretary of State shall consult a person appearing to him to be a representative of persons interested in the shooting of birds of the kind proposed to be protected by the Order.

6.3   General and specific licences

The Act also allows the killing or taking of bird species which are considered to be pests by the granting (in England) of general or specific licences. Section 16 gives the Secretary of State and/or Natural England (in practice the Secretary of State has delegated his authority to Natural England for this purpose) the power to grant such licences. As can be seen below the strict terms of a licence have to be adhered to. Section 16 of the Act specifies that licences can only be granted (whether in general or specific terms for the following reasons:

(a) for scientific, research or educational purposes;

(b) for the purpose of ringing or marking, or examining any ring or mark on, wild birds;

(c) for the purpose of conserving wild birds;

(ca) for the purposes of the re-population of an area with, or the re-introduction into an area of, wild birds, including any breeding necessary for those purposes;

(cb) for the purpose of conserving flora or fauna;

(d) for the purpose of protecting any collection of wild birds;

(e) for the purposes of falconry or aviculture;

(f) for the purposes of any public exhibition or competition;

(g) for the purposes of taxidermy;

(h) for the purpose of photography;

(i) for the purposes of preserving public health or public or air safety;

(j) for the purpose of preventing the spread of disease; or

(k) for the purposes of preventing serious damage to livestock, foodstuffs for livestock, crops, vegetables, fruit, growing timber, fisheries or inland waters, ...

In practice, grounds (i) (j) and (k) are the ones most relied upon.

It is important to realise therefore that the terms of the licence must be strictly adhered to if the law's requirements are to be met. The shooting community has for many years relied on the powers of s 16(1)(j) and 16(5) of the Act which specifically require the licence to be issued for the purposes of preventing the spread of disease. It also regularly relies on the grounds contained in the Act which allow shooting for the purposes of preventing serious damage to livestock, foodstuffs for livestock, crops, vegetables, fruit, growing timber, fisheries or inland waters.

The species which are covered by the licence include greater Canada geese, crow, doves, certain species of gulls, jackdaws, jays, magpies, fell pigeons, rooks and wood pigeons. It is not unknown for there to be prosecutions brought by the RSPCA claiming that the terms of the general licence have not been met. In particular, it is not appropriate to shoot these species relying on the general licence if one is simply shooting them for sport. In order to rely on the licence one has to be an authorised person as defined in s 27 of the Act, which means either the owner or occupier or any person authorised by the owner or occupier of the land on which the action is taken or any person authorised in writing by the local authority for the area within which the action was taken or a person authorised by

Natural England or the Environment Agency. In practice, for private citizens one has to be either the owner or occupier of the parcel of land on which one is shooting one of these species or someone authorised by him. The best practice is to have a written authorisation in one's possession so that if one is challenged one can demonstrate that one falls within the terms of a general licence.[3] It is also best practice to carry a copy of the general licence with one when one is shooting to demonstrate that one understands its terms if challenged. Failure to comply with the terms of the general licence can lead to a fine up to a level 5 and/or a 6-month custodial sentence at the election of the court.

6.4 Game species – Sunday and Christmas day

GA 1831, s 3 prevents the legal killing or taking of game as defined in s 2[4] on a Sunday or Christmas day.

It reads:

> If any person whatsoever shall kill or take any game, or use any dog, gun, net, or other engine or instrument for the purpose of killing or taking any game, on a Sunday or Christmas Day, such person shall, on conviction thereof before two justices of the peace, forfeit and pay for every such offence such sum of money, not exceeding level 1 on the standard scale, as to the said justices shall seem meet, ...

The section prevents two activities. First, the killing or taking of game *per se*. The expression 'killing or taking' is well understood and defined as a matter of construction. It is used in several other sections of the GA 1831. Second, it prevents killing or taking using a dog, gun, net or engine. This expression is used in the Offences Against the Person Act 1861 and is considered in all criminal law textbooks so is not discussed here. The reader should note that this expression is considered further in the context of the 1861 Act in para 5.5.

6.5 Game species – closed seasons

GA 1831, s 3 also allows the killing or taking of game only during specified periods of the year. It reads (as amended):

> ... if any person whatsoever shall kill or take any partridge between the first day of February and the first day of September in any year,
>
> or any pheasant between the first day of February and the first day of October in any year,

---

[3]   A suitable precedent for such an authority is set out at Appendix A6.

[4]   See Chapter 3.

or any black game (except in the county of Somerset or Devon, or in the New forest in the county of Southampton,) between the tenth day of December in any year and the twentieth day of August in the succeeding year, or in the county of Somerset or Devon, or in the New forest aforesaid, between the tenth day of December in any year and the first day of September in the succeeding year,

or any grouse commonly called red game between the tenth day of December in any year and the twelfth day of August in the succeeding year,

or any bustard between the first day of March and the first day of September in any year,

every such person shall, on conviction of any such offence before two justices of the peace, forfeit and pay for every head of game so killed or taken such sum of money, not exceeding level 1 on the standard scale, as to the said justices shall seem meet.

Note the quaint and archaic terminology used in the section and the variable closed season for black grouse (*tetrao tetrix*). It is not thought likely that there are any black grouse in those counties in any number at present if at all. Bustard became extinct in England in the early part of the 19th century and are at present subject to a project to re-establish them at present. They are undoubtedly now protected by the WCA 1981. The writer could spend much time picking over just how one might define the New Forest and whether that definition or the 1831 definition is used now, but in the circumstances it seems facile. This shows in graphic terms how archaic are our game laws and how the passing of the RRO 2007 only achieved a small modicum of reform and how much more there is to do.

The offences under s 3 are seldom prosecuted in modern times and there are relatively few reported cases on GA 1831, s 3. The only one of any importance is *Allen v Thompson*,[5] which is authority for the proposition that a snare is an engine or instrument (this section prevents the use of a dog, gun, net or other engine or instrument for the purposes of killing or taking game). It is also authority for the proposition that one may be convicted under GA 1831, s 3 for using a snare on a Sunday if it is discovered on that day, even if it was set on another day of the week. The use of snares is controlled by the WCA 1981 in any event. Readers who are involved in a prosecution under this section should also consider Offences Against the Persons Act 1861, s 31 and the cases of *Regina v Munks*[6] and *R v Cockburn*.[7] This section has very similar wording and the cases show the modern treatment of the wording by the judiciary in a

---

[5]   (1870) LR 5QB 336.

[6]   [1964] 1 QB 304.

[7]   [2008] EWCA Crim 316, [2008] 2 WLR 1274.

criminal prosecution context. It should be noted that if one takes away a live pheasant caught in a rabbit trap on one's own land, one infringes this section but one may be found innocent if one can show that one did not intend to appropriate the bird.[8]

6.6 Hares and rabbits

Hares Preservation Act 1892, s 2 prevents the sale of any part of a hare or leveret at certain times of the year. This does not amount to a prohibition on killing hares (although the GGA 1880 has closed seasons for killing ground game[9] in certain circumstances[10]). The section reads:

> It shall not be lawful during the months of March, April, May, June, or July to sell or expose for sale in any part of Great Britain any hare or leveret, and any person who during the months aforesaid shall so sell or expose for sale any hare or leveret shall be liable to a penalty not exceeding level 1 on the standard scale, including costs of conviction.

The Act does not apply to imported foreign hares.[11] Any offence under this Act is to be prosecuted summarily, ie in a Magistrates' Court.[12] Subject to this there are no closed seasons for killing or taking rabbits and hares in England and Wales. Hares are contained with the definition of game under GA 1831, s 2 and, as such, cannot be killed or taken on a Sunday or on Christmas day.[13]

6.7 Agriculture Act 1947

Section 98 of this Act allows the minster (now the Secretary of State for DEFRA) to order the destruction of certain animals or birds (details of which are given in the quotation from the section below) for certain purposes which are also set out in the quotation from the section below. The Act provides that anyone complying with a notice under this section does not commit an offence under the GA 1831 if they destroy game out of season and cannot fail to comply with the notice on that ground. It makes no mention of offences under WCA 1981, s 1.

---

[8] See *Watkins v Price* (1877) 2 JP 21.

[9] Ie rabbits and hares.

[10] See s 1(3) as amended.

[11] See Hares Preservation Act 1892, s 3.

[12] See Hares Preservation Act 1892, s 4.

[13] See GA 1831, s 3.

Section 98(1) reads:

> (1) If it appears to the Minister that it is expedient so to do for the purpose of preventing damage to crops, pasture, animal or human foodstuffs, livestock, trees, hedges, banks or any works on land, he may by notice in writing served on any person having the right so to do require that person to take, within such time as may be specified in the notice, such steps (including such steps, if any, as may be so specified) as may be necessary for the killing, taking or destruction on land so specified of such animals or birds to which this section applies as may be so specified or the eggs of such birds.

The saving provision reads:

> Provided that a requirement may be so imposed to kill or destroy game within the meaning of the Game Act 1831, at a time of year at which apart from this proviso the killing or destruction would be prohibited by section three of that Act; and for the purposes of the last foregoing subsection a person shall not be deemed not to have the right to comply with a requirement falling within this proviso by reason only that apart from this proviso compliance therewith would be prohibited as aforesaid.

The species covered by this section are set out in s 98(4), which reads:

> (4) The animals to which this section applies are rabbits, hares and other rodents, deer, foxes and moles, and the birds to which this section applies are, in relation to any area, wild birds other than those included in the First Schedule to the Protection of Birds Act 1954 as it applies in that area whether by virtue of the terms thereof ... or by virtue of an order of the Secretary of State; and this section shall apply to such other animals as may be prescribed: ...

The birds specified in Protection of Birds Act 1954, Sch 1 were subsumed in the WCA 1981 (Schs 1 and 2), which re-enacts much of what was in the 1954 Act.

6.8 Summary

For ease of comprehension a table is set out below which seeks to combine the closed seasons (and for convenience the open seasons) derived from both the GA 1831 and the WCA 1981 (see Table 6.1). If a species is not mentioned it is appropriate to check if it protected under WCA 1981, Sch 1 and is thus not capable of being legally shot or if protected by Sch 2 whether it is in season.[14] The law applies between dates in other words the closed season excludes the start and end dates.

---

[14] Schedule 2 is set out at Appendix B3.

Table 6.1: Closed and open seasons

Species	Closed season (between dates)	Open Season	Statute and section	Comments
Partridge	01.02 to 01.09	1.09 to 31.01	GA 1831, s 3	
Pheasant	01.02 to 01.10	01.10 to 01.02	GA 1831, s 3	
Black game	10.12 to 20. 08	20.08 to 10.12	GA 1831, s 3	Ie black grouse There is an exception in the counties of Somerset and Devon, and in the New Forest (county of Southampton), where the period is 10.12 to 01.09
Red Grouse	10.12 to 12.08	12.08 to 10.12	GA 1831, s 3	
Bustard	01.03 to 01.09	N/A	GA 1831, s 3	NB Bustard now protected by virtue of WCA 1981, s 1 and so this is academic
Capercaille	01.02 to 30.09	01.10 to 01.02	WCA 1981, s 2	This bird still appears to be listed in some copies of the WCA 1981 as a protected bird in Sch 1 but has been categorised as Sch 2
Woodcock	01.02 to 30.09	01.10 to 31.01	WCA 1981, s 2	

Species	*Closed season (between dates)*	*Open Season*	*Statute and section*	*Comments*
Snipe	01.02 to 11.08	12.08 to 31.01	WCA 1981, s 2	
Wild duck and wild geese	21.02 to 31.08	01.09 to 20.02	WCA 1981, s 2	But only in any area below high water mark of ordinary spring tides inland it is 01.02 to 31.8
Moorhen/ coot	1.2 to 31.8	01.09 to 31.01	WCA 1981, s 2	
Golden plover	1.2 to 31.8	01.09 to 31.01	WCA 1981, s 2	
All other species not named above but in WCA 1981, Sch 2	01.02 to 31.08	01.09 to 01.02	WCA 1981, s 2	But not those in Sch 1

7 Poaching

7.1 Introduction

Poaching is a peculiar offence, in that it is well known, but rarely prosecuted, and its essential ingredients are generally misunderstood. It is an offence that causes understandable disquiet amongst gamekeepers and landowners, while at the same time a gang of poachers rank amongst the country's greatest legendary heroes, in the form of Robin Hood's Merry Men.

It is important to recognise from the outset that poaching is not an offence akin to theft, regardless of the fact that this is how it is generally viewed.[1] Wild game, as we have seen, is not reduced to ownership unless it is killed. Because game is not owned, it cannot be stolen. Poaching then is one of a series of offences that are committed by a combination of trespass and an unlawful activity committed while trespassing. In the case of poaching, the activity is the searching for or taking of game. Poaching is not committed when a person has permission to be on land, nor is poaching committed by a trespasser who is not engaged in searching for game.

The offence of poaching as it relates to the taking of deer is dealt with in Chapter 10 and, as such, nothing more will be said about deer in this chapter. In relation to all other forms of poaching, there are four pieces of legislation that create the statutory framework for the modern offence: the two Night Poaching Acts of 1828 and 1844, the PPA 1862 and the GA 1831. In addition, the HA 2004 also creates an offence that can easily be committed by poachers.

Poaching at night has always been considered a more serious offence than poaching during the day. The reason for this relates to the pre-meditation involved in searching for game under the cover of darkness. It is harder to catch a person poaching in the dark, and there is more scope for a violent reaction to capture by the offender.

---

[1] Donaldson LJ's obiter comments in *R v David Mark Smith and William Johnson* (1982) 4 Cr App R (S) 219 would appear to run contrary to this principle. Donaldson LJ said that 'poaching is merely another form of theft and society will not tolerate it'. While the writer agrees with the noble lord's sentiment, it is important to recognise that, if poaching is a form of theft, it is a form of theft that involves stealing property that does not belong to an identifiable individual.

7.2   Night Poaching Act 1828

As a result, the first piece of legislation to place the old common law offence of poaching on a statutory footing was the NPA 1828. The Act is described in its heading as, 'An Act for the more effectual Prevention of Persons going armed by Night for the Destruction of Game'.

Section 1 of the Act creates two separate offences. The first is committed when a person *by night, unlawfully takes or destroys any game or rabbits in any land, whether open or enclosed.* The word unlawfully in the definition of this offence indicates the fact that the taking or destroying of game or rabbits is done without permission of the landowner, and is therefore the result of a trespass.

The second offence created by s 1 is committed when a person *shall by night unlawfully enter or be in any land, whether open or enclosed, with any gun, net, engine, or other instrument, for the purpose of taking or destroying game.* This is effectively an offence of going equipped to poach, but can only be committed at night, as no similar offence is created by the legislation dealing with daytime poaching. The usefulness of this second offence is that, when a gamekeeper catches a trespasser equipped for poaching on land where he has no permission to be, it is not necessary to prove that he had actually taken or destroyed any game in order to prosecute him for the offence of poaching.

The current version of this Act allows on summary conviction for a level 3 fine on the standard scale. This means the maximum fine currently stands at £1000. As the two s 1 offences are summary offences, an offender must be charged or summonsed within 6 months of the offence being committed.

Section 2 provides a power to any landowner, or occupier of land, or lord of the manor, as well as the gamekeepers and servants of any of those people, to apprehend anyone committing an offence created by the Act. The offender can be apprehended on the land where the offence was committed or anywhere that he has fled to following a pursuit. When apprehended, the offender must be handed over to the custody of the police, in order to be taken before the court. Section 2 also creates an offence of assaulting, or offering violence with a weapon, to anyone using the power to apprehend an offender. This is a summary offence with a maximum level 4 fine or 6 months' imprisonment.

There is a further offence, created by s 9 of the Act, which is committed by a group of three or more people committing the s 1 offences together. The aggravating feature of a group committing the offences means that, on conviction, there is a higher, level 4 maximum fine or 6 months' imprisonment.

Section 12 of the Act defines night as the period between the first hour after sunset and the first hour before sunrise, while s 13 provides a definition of game:

> For the purposes of this Act the word 'game' shall be deemed to include hares, pheasants, partridges, grouse, heath or moor game, black game, and bustards.

7.3   Night Poaching Act 1844

In 1844 a second Night Poaching Act achieved Royal Assent. The purpose of the second Act was to make it easier to apprehend persons engaged in night poaching. The second Act extended the provisions of the first Act to encompass offences committed on the public highway. This enabled landowners and their servants to apprehend poachers on the public highway near their land, and prevented the poachers from claiming that any game found on them was taken on the highway. Where public rights of way ran across private land, this was an extremely important development.

7.4   Poaching Prevention Act 1862

In 1862 an Act was passed to deal with daytime poaching. The PPA 1862 was very different from the Night Poaching Acts that had preceded it. For a start, the definition of game contained within s 1 of the Act was different, in that it defines game as including:

> any one or more hares, pheasants, partridges, eggs of pheasants and partridges, woodcocks, snipes, rabbits, grouse, black or moor game, and eggs of grouse, black or moor game.

Section 1 of the Act also deals entirely differently with daytime poaching as an offence. The section empowers police constables rather than landowners or their servants to stop and search suspected poachers. The section allows constables to search any person:

> whom he may have good cause to suspect of coming from any land where he shall have been unlawfully in search or pursuit of game, or any person aiding or abetting such person, and having in his possession any game unlawfully obtained, or any gun, part of gun, ... and also to stop and search any cart or other conveyance in or upon which such constable or peace officer shall have good cause to suspect that any such game or any such article or thing is being carried by any such person.

Section 1 empowers the constable to seize any game, or gun or part of a gun found during the course of a search.

The section goes on to create an offence of having obtained game unlawfully and an offence of having used a gun in the unlawful killing or taking of game. In addition, it is an offence to have been an accessory to either of these offences. The punishment, on summary conviction, is a level 3 fine.

The utility of the PPA 1862 derives from the fact that it allowed police constables to stop and search poachers and their associates, and to seize their weapons, where they had grounds to suspect that poaching was intended. This is clearly a much wider power than was given to landowners and their servants, who could only apprehend a poacher who was equipped for poaching and had trespassed on land at night. As stated above, however, there is no offence of going equipped to poach during the day, and the PPA 1862 only makes daytime poaching itself an offence.

7.5   Game Act 1831

The GA 1831 also creates an offence of daytime poaching. Section 30 of that Act makes it an offence punishable by a level 3 fine to:

> commit any trespass by entering or being in the daytime upon any land in search or pursuit of game, or woodcocks, snipes, ... or conies.

If four or more people commit this offence together, the fine is increased to level 4.

Section 31 of the Act empowers the person with the right to kill game on the land, or the occupier, or their gamekeepers or servants, to require anyone trespassing in pursuit of game to leave the land after providing his name and address. Should the trespasser refuse to provide his name and address, or should he make up an imaginary address, or should he return to the land having been required to leave, he can be lawfully apprehended and taken to court where he will face a level 1 fine on conviction.

Section 32 also creates an offence whereby five or more people, one of whom must be armed with a gun, use violence or intimidation to prevent a person from requiring them to quit the land. Such an offence is punishable with a level 5 fine.

Section 41 requires that any prosecution brought under the GA 1831 is commenced within 3 months of the commission of an offence.

7.6   Case law

In the main, the leading cases on poaching date back to the 19th century and, as such, provide a historical insight into the state of criminal jurisprudence at the time. The case of *Brown v Turner*[2] highlights the evidential sufficiency required to successfully prosecute a poaching case. Four defendants in that case were apprehended by a police constable early on a Sunday morning on a high road near Braintree in Essex. The first defendant was found with five recently killed wild rabbits and an iron spud in his pockets. The second defendant was found with a recently used net, suitable for catching rabbits, some rabbit fur and blood on his cuffs. The police constable later discovered that the third defendant had sold a wild dead rabbit on the same morning at a beer house. The only evidence against the fourth defendant was that he was in company with the first three defendants and had dirty shoes.

It was argued on behalf of the defendants that the GA 1831 required the men to have taken the rabbits unlawfully on land that they had entered as trespassers, and that, as there was no evidence before the court that the defendants had ever been off the public highway, it was not proper for the magistrates to infer a trespass without evidence. The court found that the circumstances of the first three defendants being found together at the time in possession of the articles found on them was sufficient for the magistrates to have inferred that they had been poaching. The fourth defendant was acquitted.

The case of *Brown v Turner* was followed, with reservations, by the case of *Evans v Botterill and others*.[3] In that case a group of men were stopped by constables early on a Sunday morning and found to be in possession of dead rabbits, hares and nets capable of being used to catch rabbits and hares. The magistrates initially acquitted the defendants on the grounds that they felt that evidence should have been provided to show that either the defendants had been on land unlawfully or that they had used the nets unlawfully. The constables appealed.

Blackburn J, in his judgment, said the following:

> It is sufficient if there was evidence leading to the conclusion that the persons charged had been on any land in search or pursuit of game, or that they had used a net or other instrument for killing or taking any game. But I wish to draw attention to this, that the language of sect. 2, creating the offence, is 'if such person shall have obtained such game by unlawfully going on any land

---

[2]   *John Brown, Joseph Melbourne, Henry Chapman, and Walter Peters v Charles Turner* (1863) 13 CBNS 485, [1863] 143 ER 192.

[3]   *Evans, Appellant v Botterill and Others* (1863) 3 B&S 787, 122 ER 294.

in search or pursuit of game, or shall have used any such article or thing as aforesaid for unlawfully killing or taking game,' and the justices ought not to convict unless they are satisfied that the parties charged have been on land, or have used nets or other instruments for those purposes. The evidence in the present case is sufficient, though not conclusive, to justify a conviction for obtaining game by unlawfully going on land, and also for using nets for unlawfully taking game. The force of the evidence may depend very much upon the place and hour where persons are met. But there is no presumption of law or fact, merely because persons are possessed of game or nets at a suspicious time and place, that they have been guilty of either of the offences.

Mellor J agreed that, although there was strong evidence in the case on which the magistrates might have inferred unlawful activity, they were not bound to do so.

In a further case, *Jenkin and Dennis v King*,[4] two defendants were convicted having been found with a net and a lurcher. A constable gave evidence that he had heard the lurcher yelping when the two men were trespassing on a nearby piece of land, as if it were hunting. The convictions were upheld on the basis that the men were attempting to poach, albeit unsuccessfully.

7.7   Summary

*   Poaching is a combination of an act of trespass and the unlawful activity of searching for or taking game.

*   The offence is considered more serious when committed at night.

*   Landowners, their servants, gamekeepers and the police have statutory powers to prevent poaching.

*   Police powers include the power to stop and search individuals suspected of poaching and to seize items from them associated with the commission of the offence.

*   Courts are entitled to rely on circumstantial evidence, such as the possession of nets, guns, carcasses, etc that give rise to an inference that an individual has been poaching, in order to convict.

*   Searching for game is sufficient to basis a conviction for poaching.

---

[4]   *Jenkin and Dennis v King* (1871–72) LR 7, QB 478, 24 April 1872, QBD.

8 Hunting

8.1 Introduction

By far the most controversial aspect of game sports law is the law as it affects hunting. When the HA 2004 came into force on 18 February 2005, it appeared, initially, to have banned hunting with dogs in the United Kingdom, save in prescribed circumstances. Following the High Court decision in the linked cases of *DPP v Wright* and *R on the application of Scott, Heard and Summersgill v Taunton Deane Magistrates' Court*,[1] it appears that on proper analysis the Act has created a distinct offence of hunting with dogs, the particular elements of which distinguish it from the lawful pursuit of 'exempt hunting' and other lawful activities such as trail hunting.

8.2 Hunting Act 2004 – history

It is perhaps unsurprising that the HA 2004 remains controversial, considering the length of time that it took to bring a piece of legislation restricting hunting onto the statute books. Historically, hunting had been specifically exempted from legislation intended to promote animal welfare. Animal welfare legislation dates back to Martin's Act 'to prevent the cruel and improper treatment of cattle' passed in 1822. A series of Acts of Parliament intended to promote animal welfare and protect animals from suffering were passed during the 1800s. This legislation affected domesticated animals in human care rather than wild animals. The Wild Animals in Captivity Protection Act 1900 was intended to afford protection to those captive wild animals that were outside the protection of the previous legislation. Section 4 of the Act specifically disapplied this protection to animals that were hunted or coursed so long as they were not released in a mutilated or injured state.[2] The Protection of Animals Act 1911, the Protection of Badgers Act 1992 (PBA 1992) and the Wild Mammals (Protection) Act 1996 all contained similar exemptions.

---

[1]   [2009] EWHC 105 (Admin), 2009 WL 289265.

[2]   For more information on the development of animal welfare legislation, see Mike Radford, *Animal Welfare Law in Britain: Regulation and Responsibility* (Oxford University Press, 2001).

A series of Private Members' Bills introduced during the 20th century, intended to ban hunting and coursing, failed to become law. The most famous of the Private Members' Bills, the 1997 Wild Mammals (Hunting with Dogs) Bill, introduced by Worcester MP Michael Foster, received the support of 411 MPs but ran out of parliamentary time and had to be abandoned. For those supporters of Michael Foster's Bill, its failure to produce legislation represented a failure of the democratic process to ensure that the will of Parliament was reflected in statute. For the opponents of the Bill, it represented a stay of execution from what they perceived to be an unwarranted attack on the rural economy and a cherished way of life.

The task of balancing the desire to ban hunting, perceived by its opponents to cause suffering in the name of sport, with the need to protect that part of the rural economy that depended upon hunting for its survival was made more difficult by the lack of reliable data on either side. This lack of definitive evidence undermined arguments put by the pro-hunting lobby, in that it was difficult for them to point to firm figures relating to how many people depended upon hunting for their income and what the real effect of a ban was likely to be. It also undermined the anti-hunting lobby, who were unable to substantiate the claim that hunting was cruel by reference to definitive scientific studies.

In 1999 Jack Straw, the Home Secretary, appointed a Committee of Inquiry, under Lord Burns,[3] to inquire into:

> the practical aspects of different types of hunting with dogs and its impact on the rural economy, agriculture and pest control, the social and cultural life of the countryside, the management and conservation of wildlife, and animal welfare in particular areas of England and Wales;
>
> the consequences for these issues of any ban on hunting with dogs; and
>
> how any ban might be implemented.

The Burns Inquiry did not produce the definitive answer that may have been hoped for. The Report of the Inquiry[4] concluded that hunting did significantly compromise the welfare of foxes, but were not convinced that hunting was worse in terms of animal welfare than other legal means of predator control such as shooting foxes with shotguns during the day or snaring. The Report accepted that in some areas the welfare of foxes would be adversely affected by a ban unless the use of dogs was allowed to flush the foxes from cover.

---

[3]   Committee of Inquiry into Hunting with Dogs in England and Wales (the Burns Inquiry).

[4]   Lord Burns, *Final Report of the Committee of Inquiry into Hunting with Dogs in England and Wales* (The Stationery Office, 2000).

The Report was clear that it was not possible to put a precise figure on the numbers of people who were likely to lose their jobs if hunting were banned, and anticipated some significant effects on the rural economy in the short to medium term. It was estimated that the effects would be offset by increased expenditure on other areas of rural life. It was recognised that the negative impacts of a ban would be particularly resented because they would be viewed as unnecessary by many of those affected, and as an avoidable addition to other problems facing the farming community. It was also recognised that, in more isolated communities, hunting acts as a significant cohesive force, encouraging mutual support. The Report predicted that many people in such communities value hunting as an expression of a traditional, rural way of life and would strongly resent what they would see as an unnecessary and ill-informed interference with it. As a result a ban on hunting would increase their sense of alienation.

The Report concluded that a ban might be open to challenge under the European Convention on Human Rights on a number of grounds, but that a Bill framed with a requirement to prove unnecessary suffering may prove more resistant to challenge than an outright ban. The Report also concluded that consideration should be given as to whether any ban would be manifestly unjust due to the activities that were caught by it and those activities that were not.[5]

Following the Burns Inquiry, the Government introduced a Bill that included a number of potential options including an outright ban, a system of licensing and the continuation of self-regulation. The Bill passed through several stages of amendment, but never passed the Lords, and the current Act, containing the outright ban, was made law as a result of the Government's highly controversial use of the Parliament Act. Prior to the 2010 general election the Conservative Party made a manifesto commitment to a free vote on the repeal of the HA 2004. It remains to be seen, at the time of writing, when and if that free vote will take place.

8.3   The legislation

The HA 2004 is described in its title as 'an Act to make provision about hunting wild mammals with dogs; to prohibit hare coursing; and for connected purposes'. It is worth noting that this description appears to be consistent with the findings in the *Scott, Heard and Summersgill* case[6] that

---

5   Lord Burns, *Final Report of the Committee of Inquiry into Hunting with Dogs in England and Wales* (The Stationery Office, 2000).

6   [2009] EWHC 105 (Admin), 2009 WL 289265.

the term hunting can be applied both to unlawful hunting and lawful exempt hunting, as well as to other lawful activities such as drag hunting, trail hunting, etc that do not involve the pursuit of a mammal.

8.4   The offence of 'unlawful hunting'

Section 1 of the Act creates the main offence of hunting a wild mammal with dogs. Section 1 states that a person commits an offence if he hunts a wild mammal with a dog, unless his hunting is exempt.

Section 2 provides that hunting is exempt if it is within a class specified in Sch 1 and further allows that the Secretary of State may by order amend Sch 1 so as to vary a class of exempt hunting.

A definition of hunting is contained at s 11(2), which states:

> (2) For the purposes of this Act a reference to a person hunting a wild mammal with a dog includes, in particular, any case where—
>
> > (a) a person engages or participates in the pursuit of a wild mammal, and
> >
> > (b) one or more dogs are employed in that pursuit (whether or not by him and whether or not under his control or direction).

The inclusion of the words 'in particular' in the definition has led the League Against Cruel Sports to argue in a series of cases at trial that the definition contained in s 11(2) is only a partial definition and does not prevent activities outside the definition being caught by s 1. In particular, it was argued that a person 'searching' for a mammal to hunt would be guilty of the offence of unlawful hunting even though, at the time, he was not engaged in the pursuit of a wild mammal. It would appear that the *Scott, Heard and Summersgill* case has put an end to that particular line of argument. As a result it is difficult to think of any activity that would not involve a person engaging in the pursuit of an identifiable wild mammal but that would fall under the definition of 'hunting.'

8.5   Lawful 'exempt hunting'

Section 4 provides a statutory defence to a person charged with an offence under s 1 who reasonably believed that his hunting was exempt.

It is worth, at this stage, considering the exemptions contained within Sch 1 in order to get an idea of the sort of lawful hunting that is not caught by the offence set out in s 1 of the Act.

Schedule 1 contains a series of exemptions, many of which contain express conditions that a person is required to fulfil if their hunting is to remain lawful. Schedule 1, para 1 is entitled 'Stalking and flushing out'.

8.6   Stalking and flushing out

Paragraph 1(1) states that:

(1) Stalking a wild mammal, or flushing it out of cover, is exempt hunting if the conditions in this paragraph are satisfied.

Paragraph 1(2) states that:

(2) The first condition is that the stalking or flushing out is undertaken for the purpose of—

(a) preventing or reducing serious damage which the wild mammal would otherwise cause—

(i)   to livestock,

(ii)   to game birds or wild birds (within the meaning of section 27 of the Wildlife and Countryside Act 1981 (c. 69)),

(iii) to food for livestock,

(iv)   to crops (including vegetables and fruit),

(v)   to growing timber,

(vi)   to fisheries,

(vii) to other property, or

(viii) to the biological diversity of an area (within the meaning of the United Nations Environmental Programme Convention on Biological Diversity of 1992),

(b) obtaining meat to be used for human or animal consumption, or

(c) participation in a field trial.

Paragraph 1(3) provides a definition of field trial.

Paragraph 1(4) contains the second condition which is that:

(4) ... the stalking or flushing out takes place on land—

(a) which belongs to the person doing the stalking or flushing out, or

(b) which he has been given permission to use for the purpose by the occupier or, in the case of unoccupied land, by a person to whom it belongs.

Paragraph 1(5) contains the third condition which is that the stalking or flushing does not involve the use of more than two dogs.

Paragraph 1(6) contains the fourth condition which is that the stalking or flushing out does not involve the use of a dog below ground otherwise than in accordance with para 2 of the Schedule.

Paragraph 1(7) contains the fifth condition which is that:

(a)   reasonable steps are taken for the purpose of ensuring that as soon as possible after being found or flushed out the wild mammal is shot dead by a competent person, and

(b)   in particular, each dog used in the stalking or flushing out is kept under sufficiently close control to ensure that it does not prevent or obstruct achievement of the objective in paragraph (a).

We can therefore see, for example, that a person is entitled to flush a wild mammal from cover using no more than two dogs where he has the permission of the landowner; where the reason for his hunting is to reduce the damage that the wild mammal would otherwise cause to crops; provided that he has taken reasonable steps to ensure that the wild mammal is shot dead by a competent person as soon as possible after being flushed from cover, and that each of his dogs is kept under sufficiently close control in order to ensure that it does not interfere with the competent person's ability to shoot the wild mammal dead as soon as possible.

8.7   Use of dogs below ground

Paragraph 2 relates to the use of dogs below ground to protect birds for shooting and makes it lawful to use a dog below ground in the course of stalking or flushing out if its conditions are satisfied.

The first condition is that the stalking or flushing out is undertaken for the purpose of preventing or reducing serious damage to game birds or wild birds (within the meaning of WCA 1981, s 27) which a person is keeping or preserving for the purpose of their being shot.

The second condition is that the person doing the stalking or flushing out has with him written evidence:

(i)   that the land on which the stalking or flushing out takes place belongs to him, or

(ii)   that he has been given permission to use that land for the purpose by the occupier or, in the case of unoccupied land, by a person to whom it belongs, and

(b)   makes the evidence immediately available for inspection by a constable who asks to see it

It is worth noting therefore that anyone seeking to remain within this exemption must carry with them written evidence relating to the exemption.

The third condition is that the stalking or flushing out does not involve the use of more than one dog below ground at any one time.

Paragraph 2(5) provides further conditions under this exemption as follows:

(a) reasonable steps are taken for the purpose of ensuring that as soon as possible after being found the wild mammal is flushed out from below ground,

(b) reasonable steps are taken for the purpose of ensuring that as soon as possible after being flushed out from below ground the wild mammal is shot dead by a competent person,

(c) in particular, the dog is brought under sufficiently close control to ensure that it does not prevent or obstruct achievement of the objective in paragraph (b),

(d) reasonable steps are taken for the purpose of preventing injury to the dog, and

(e) the manner in which the dog is used complies with any code of practice which is issued or approved for the purpose of this paragraph by the Secretary of State.

It is worth noting that this exemption requires reasonable steps to be taken for the purpose of preventing injury to the dog that is used below ground. The RSPCA has historically also used animal welfare legislation to bring cases where there is an allegation of injury to dogs used below ground.

8.8   Rats, rabbits and retrieving hares

Paragraphs 3, 4 and 5 relate to exemptions for hunting rats, rabbits and retrieving hares that have been shot. Each of these activities is lawful if it is undertaken on land which belongs to the hunter or which he has been given permission to hunt on by the owner or occupier of the land.

8.9   Falconry

In addition, para 6 exempts flushing a wild mammal from cover for the purposes of falconry if the same conditions are met.

8.10 Mammals that have escaped or been released

Paragraph 7 allows for the hunting of a wild mammal which has escaped or been released from captivity or confinement if the following conditions are satisfied:

(2) The first condition is that the hunting takes place—

(a) on land which belongs to the hunter,

(b) on land which he has been given permission to use for the purpose by the occupier or, in the case of unoccupied land, by a person to whom it belongs, or

(c) with the authority of a constable.

(3) The second condition is that—

(a) reasonable steps are taken for the purpose of ensuring that as soon as possible after being found the wild mammal is recaptured or shot dead by a competent person, and

(b) in particular, each dog used in the hunt is kept under sufficiently close control to ensure that it does not prevent or obstruct achievement of the objective in paragraph (a).

(4) The third condition is that the wild mammal—

(a) was not released for the purpose of being hunted, and

(b) was not, for that purpose, permitted to escape.

8.11 Rescue

Paragraph 8 provides for the rescue of a wild mammal in the event that it has suffered an injury. The conditions relating to this are as follows:

(2) The first condition is that the hunter reasonably believes that the wild mammal is or may be injured.

(3) The second condition is that the hunting is undertaken for the purpose of relieving the wild mammal's suffering.

(4) The third condition is that the hunting does not involve the use of more than two dogs.

(5) The fourth condition is that the hunting does not involve the use of a dog below ground.

(6) The fifth condition is that the hunting takes place—

(a) on land which belongs to the hunter,

(b) on land which he has been given permission to use for the purpose by the occupier or, in the case of unoccupied land, by a person to whom it belongs, or

(c) with the authority of a constable.

(7) The sixth condition is that—

(a) reasonable steps are taken for the purpose of ensuring that as soon as possible after the wild mammal is found appropriate action (if any) is taken to relieve its suffering, and

(b) in particular, each dog used in the hunt is kept under sufficiently close control to ensure that it does not prevent or obstruct achievement of the objective in paragraph(a).

(8) The seventh condition is that the wild mammal was not harmed for the purpose of enabling it to be hunted in reliance upon this paragraph.

8.12   Research and observation

Paragraph 9 relates to the exemption covering research and observation and contains the following conditions:

(2) The first condition is that the hunting is undertaken for the purpose of or in connection with the observation or study of the wild mammal.

(3) The second condition is that the hunting does not involve the use of more than two dogs.

(4) The third condition is that the hunting does not involve the use of a dog below ground.

(5) The fourth condition is that the hunting takes place on land—

(a) which belongs to the hunter, or

(b) which he has been given permission to use for the purpose by the occupier or, in the

(c) case of unoccupied land, by a person to whom it belongs.

(6) The fifth condition is that each dog used in the hunt is kept under sufficiently close control to ensure that it does not injure the wild mammal.

8.13   Overview of lawful hunting

We see then that lawful hunting falls into two categories. The hunting of rats and rabbits, the retrieval of hares, flushing for the purposes of falconry and hunting in order to recapture a wild animal are all lawful no matter how many dogs are employed in the course of the hunt. If, however, one wishes to use a dog below ground to flush wild mammals to guns, only one dog can lawfully be used at a time. Similarly, if the purpose of lawful hunting is stalking or flushing out above ground, or the rescue of a wild mammal that is injured or thought to be injured, or in order to observe or study a wild mammal, then a maximum of two dogs can be used at any one time.

As we can see below, following the case of *Scott, Heard and Summersgill*, if an individual is to be prosecuted in regard to an allegation of unlawful hunting, once the issue of exempt hunting is raised on the evidence either by the defendant or the nature of the facts of the case, it is for the prosecution to prove to the criminal standard that the individual's activities were outside of the exemption relating to his particular case. So, for example, if an individual was out hunting rabbits, and said in interview that this was the purpose of his hunting, it would be for the prosecution to show that either he was not hunting rabbits or that he did not have the appropriate permission to fulfil the condition set out in para 4. Alternatively, if the only prosecution evidence in the case related to the hunting of rabbits, even where the defendant made no comment in interview, it is the writer's view that the issue of exempt hunting under para 4 would clearly be raised by the nature of the facts of the case, and the prosecution would still be required to prove that the exemption did not apply.

8.14   Miscellaneous offences

HA 2004, s 3 makes it an offence for a person to knowingly permit land which belongs to him to be used for the purposes of unlawful hunting. Section 3 also makes it an offence for a person to knowingly permit a dog that belongs to him to be used in the course of unlawful hunting. Section 11(3) defines land as belonging to a person where he owns the land, manages or controls the land or occupies the land. Section 11(4) defines a dog as belonging to a person where he owns the dog, is in charge of the dog or has control of the dog.

Section 5 creates the offence of hare coursing. A 'hare coursing event' is defined by s 5(3) as a competition in which dogs are, by the use of live hares, assessed as to skill in hunting hares.

8.15   Enforcement

Part 2 of the Act is entitled Enforcement. Section 6 provides that the offences created by the Act are summary matters carrying a maximum fine not exceeding level 5 on the standard scale.

Section 8 enables a constable who reasonably suspects that a person is committing or has committed an offence under Part 1 to stop and search the person or any vehicle, animal or thing that he is control of. It also enables the constable to seize and detain the vehicle, animal or thing, and to enter land, premises and vehicles,without a warrant.

Section 9 allows a court which convicts a person of any offence under Part 1 of the Act to order the forfeiture of any dog or hunting article which was used in the commission of the offence or was in the person's possession at the time of the offence. It also allows the court to make provisions regarding the treatment of the dog or article and, where the court fails to specify how the dog or article is to be treated, allows the police to arrange for its destruction or disposal. The court can also order any person to surrender the dog or article to a constable, and order the return of the dog or article on application made by a person with an interest in the dog, vehicle or article before its destruction or disposal. A person commits an offence if he fails to comply with a forfeiture order or fails to cooperate with a step taken for the purpose of giving effect to the order.

8.16 Bodies corporate

Section 10 provides that a body corporate may commit an offence under the Act with the consent or connivance of an officer of the body and, under such circumstances, the officer as well as the body corporate shall be guilty of an offence. At the time of writing no offences have been prosecuted under s 10.

8.17 Case law

The two most important decisions relating to the HA 2004 are to be found in *R (on the Application of the Countryside Alliance and others) v the Attorney General*[7] and the linked cases of *DPP v Wright* and *R on the application of Scott Heard and Summersgill v Taunton Deane Magistrates' Court*.[8] The *Countryside Alliance* case is important because it related to a challenge to the legitimacy of the HA 2004 itself, whereas the decision in the *Scott, Heard and Summersgill* case ensured that the new offence of unlawful hunting could not be interpreted too widely so as to catch lawful hunting, and further ensured that the presumption of innocence was not undermined in relation to HA 2004 cases.

---

[7]   [2007] UKHL 52.

[8]   [2009] EWHC 105 (Admin), 2009 WL 289265.

8.18   The Countryside Alliance case

Judgment was handed down in the *Countryside Alliance* case on 28 November 2007. The House of Lords, in its judicial capacity, heard cases brought by two groups of claimants that questioned the legal basis of an Act that had never been passed by the Lords sitting in its legislative capacity.

The first group of claimants, headed by the Countryside Alliance, claimed that their human rights were infringed by the HA 2004. Their claim was brought under European Convention of Human Rights, Arts 8, 11, and 14, and First Protocol, Art 1.

The second group of claimants brought actions on the basis that the HA 2004 was inconsistent with EC Treaty, Arts 28 and 49.

The court considered, first, whether each set of claimants' rights had been interfered with and, second, whether such interference was justifiable. The main aspect of the first group of claimants' case was the interference with their Art 8 rights. These included their right to private life and autonomy, their right to a cultural lifestyle, the peaceful enjoyment of their homes and the right not to be deprived of their home and livelihood. The first group of claimants also argued that their right to the freedom of peaceful assembly was undermined by the HA 2004. In addition, they argued that Art 14 protected them against discrimination in the way in which their rights were protected.

The second group of claimants argued that the HA 2004 put restrictions on their right to trade freely within the European Union.

The court was not persuaded by any of the individual arguments raised and dismissed the appeals of both sets of claimants. For those readers who are interested in European jurisprudence the judgments will not appear surprising.

The European Court of Human Rights (ECHR) finally rejected complaints made to it following on from the House of Lords' decision.[9] The ECHR found that the applicants' Art 8 rights were not adversely affected as hunting was a public activity and the hunting community could not be regarded as an ethnic or national minority. The ECHR also found that the concept of home did not include the land over which sport was practised or allowed to be practised; no evidence was provided of anyone who was likely to lose their homes; and finally that the court was not convinced that the ban on unlawful hunting had created serious difficulties for earning one's living.

---

[9]   *Friend v the United Kingdom* (Application No 16072/06), and *Countryside Alliance and Others v the United Kingdom* (Application No 27809/08).

The ECHR also found that the applicants' Art 11 rights had not been compromised as the hunting ban did not prevent or restrict the right of assembly in order to engage in drag or trail hunting. The ECHR held that the ban had been introduced following extensive debate in Parliament.

With regard to the First Protocol, Art 1 arguments advanced by the applicants, the ECHR also rejected the argument that businesses had been arbitrarily or unreasonably deprived of the financial benefit of hunting without compensation and on that basis rejected this complaint.

8.19   The Scott, Heard and Summersgill case

The *Scott, Heard and Summersgill* case dealt with two fundamental questions concerning the prosecution of hunting offences. The first question related to the operation of Magistrates Court Act 1980, s 101. Section 101 allows for the burden of proof to be shifted from the prosecution to the defence in certain limited circumstances where a defendant claims a statutory exemption from prosecution. Due to the language of the HA 2004, the question was raised in relation to exempt hunting. The High Court was asked to determine:

> Whether the combined effect of s.101 of the Magistrates' Courts Act 1980, and the provisions of the Hunting Act 2004, are such as to place a burden on the defendant to prove the exemptions set out in sch.1 to the Hunting Act 2004?

The second question arose from an evidential difficulty that the League Against Cruel Sports encountered when it first began prosecuting cases under the HA 2004. The difficulty was that, while it was easy to obtain a great deal of evidence of people on horseback in red coats riding to hounds, it was much more difficult to obtain video footage of people actively pursuing identifiable wild mammals. This difficulty was exacerbated by the fact that the League brought prosecutions against hunt staff, rather than followers. This may have been partly because it was easier to identify hunt staff than followers, and partly for political reasons. Whatever the reason, there was no guarantee that a member of hunt staff would be in the vicinity when a wild mammal was filmed. Therefore, even if hounds were seen to be in pursuit of the mammal, it would not necessarily have provided evidence that a member of hunt staff was engaging or participating in that pursuit.

The way in which the League sought to deal with this difficulty was to argue that HA 2004, s 11(2), which provided a definition of unlawful hunting, did not contain a complete and exhaustive definition of unlawful hunting. Section 11(2) states that:

(2) For the purposes of this Act a reference to a person hunting a wild mammal with a dog includes, in particular, any case where—

(a) a person engages or participates in the pursuit of a wild mammal, and

(b) one or more dogs are employed in that pursuit (whether or not by him and whether or not under his control or direction).

The League argued that, due to the inclusion of the word 'includes' in the definition, s11(2) must be read as containing one example of possible unlawful hunting, rather than a complete statement of the elements of the offence. Clearly, this argument was likely to lead to a high degree of uncertainty as to what other activity, not contained within s 11(2), could result in a person being convicted of unlawful hunting.

The League argued that the offence of unlawful hunting could be committed by a person who was merely searching for a mammal to hunt, rather than actively engaged in the pursuit of a wild mammal. The strength of this argument rested on the general usage of the terms 'hunting for' and 'searching for' as synonyms. The weakness of the argument was linked to the fact that the mischief that the HA 2004 sought to deal with was the infliction of distress on wild mammals for the purpose of sport. Clearly, there was no possibility of any distress being caused to a mammal until it was being pursued. Criminalising people for riding around looking for an animal to hunt, even if it could be proved that this was what they were doing, was always likely to be stretching any legitimate purpose underpinning the Act to breaking point. Apart from anything else, there has always been a reluctance in English law to criminalise behaviour before a decision has clearly been made in the mind of a defendant to go through with the commission of an offence.

Nonetheless, the second question that the High Court had to determine was: 'Whether the term "hunt" a wild mammal with a dog used in s.1 of the Hunting Act 2004 includes the activity of searching for a wild animal for the purpose of stalking or flushing it'.

The court was asked to determine the two questions in relation to two linked cases. The *Wright* case involved Anthony Wright, the Huntsman of the Exmoor Foxhounds, who was the first person to be convicted of unlawful hunting. His conviction was overturned in the Exeter Crown Court. The *Wright* case was a review of the judge's stated reasons for overturning the conviction.

It is unlikely that the Crown Prosecution Service would have proceeded to appeal the *Wright* case by way of case stated, were it not for the fact that the High Court had also given permission, extremely unusually, for the defendants in the *Scott, Heard and Summersgill* case to judicially review a binding interim decision made in the magistrates' court. Normally, a decision made by magistrates cannot be reviewed by a higher court before the end of a trial. The *Scott, Heard and Summersgill* case involved the Master of the Devon and Somerset Staghounds, Maurice Scott, and two members of hunt staff, Peter Heard and Donald Summersgill. Unusually in their case it was decided that, due to the general importance of the questions to other defendants facing trial on similar issues, and the very defined nature of the questions posed, a binding decision made at Taunton Dean Magistrates' Court could be reviewed prior to their trial being heard.

The case was heard in the High Court by Sir Anthony May, the President of the Queen's Bench Division, and Maddison J.

In relation to the first question, the court carefully considered both the question of the operation of Magistrates Court Act 1980, s 101 and the question of when it was legitimate to reverse the burden of proof in a criminal case. Initially, the court held that an HA 2004 offence was not to be considered in the same vein as liquor licensing offences and other similar offences where a particular act, such as selling intoxicating liquor, is prohibited, leaving it for the defendant to prove on balance of probabilities that he was in possession of a licence that allowed him to perform the otherwise prohibited act at the time of the alleged offence.

The court went on to consider that the HA 2004 created a set of rights relating to lawful hunting. By allowing that exempt hunting was lawful, the court concluded that the Act was bestowing the right to hunt lawfully. As such, it would not be appropriate to treat lawful hunting as unlawful until the defendant proved that he was within a particular exemption. The court found that it would not be impossible for the prosecution to achieve a conviction whilst still discharging the normal burden of proof. In his judgment, Sir Anthony May concluded that:

> we are clear that, if s.1 and sch.1 of the 2004 Act are to be construed as imposing a legal burden of proof on the defendant, that would be an oppressive, disproportionate, unfair, and in particular unnecessary intrusion upon the presumption of innocence in art.6 of the Convention.

The court dismissed the claims made on behalf of the Crown that it would be impossible to prosecute HA 2004 cases if the burden of proof was not shifted to the defendant. In its judgment the court found that the answer to the first question was no, but that there was an evidential burden on the defendant to raise the question of an exemption if such a question was not clearly raised on the facts of the case.

In relation to the second question, the court found that the legislative purpose of the HA 2004 was:

the composite one of preventing or reducing unnecessary suffering to wild mammals overlaid by a moral viewpoint that causing suffering to animals for sport is unethical and should, so far as practical and proportionate, be stopped.

As a result, the court found that:

A wild mammal which is never identified as a quarry does not suffer. If it is said that searching for a wild mammal has a potential for causing suffering to wild mammals generally, an answer is that hunting wild mammals is not banned absolutely and searching for them for the purpose of exempt hunting is permitted.

Based on this reasoning, the court held that searching for an animal to hunt was not unlawful hunting. The court was careful to point out that the offence of unlawful hunting was fact-specific, and did not attempt to define exactly what 'hunting' was for the purposes of the Act. Despite this, the writer suspects that, in order to prove an individual is hunting unlawfully, it will be necessary to provide evidence of an individual actively engaging in the pursuit of a wild mammal with dogs. It would appear clear from the judgment in the *Scott, Heard and Summersgill* case that, in the event that a dog pursues a mammal and the people around the dog attempt to call it off or are not aware that it is pursuing a mammal, no offence has been committed. The case makes clear that unlawful hunting is not a strict liability offence.

8.20   Covert surveillance and hunting

One interesting legal aspect of hunting that, at the time of writing has yet to be fully explored, is the manner in which evidence relating to allegations of unlawful hunting and associated activities has been obtained and presented in criminal courts. Unlike other criminal allegations, allegations involving HA 2004 or PBA 1992 offences are not mainly the preserve of state bodies such as the police and the Crown Prosecution Service. The majority of the investigations into such offences are conducted by non-governmental organisations such as the League Against Cruel Sports, the International Fund for Animal Welfare, the RSPCA and local badger groups and organisations. This appears to be an extension of the current state of affairs that, although a charity with no statutory powers or duties to investigate or prosecute offences, the RSPCA has largely taken on the state function of the investigation and prosecution of animal welfare offences.

The effect of the private nature of the investigation of hunting and badger-related offences is that it is unclear to what extent, if any, some of the activities undertaken as part of such investigation are authorised or indeed lawful in its strictest sense. An unreported case in Bournemouth

Magistrates' Court[10] highlighted this consideration. The defendant had been summonsed in regard to an allegation of unlawful interference with a badger sett contrary to the PBA 1992. During the course of proceedings it transpired that the allegation arose from an extensive investigation involving the South Dorset Hunt conducted by the League Against Cruel Sports and a local badger group. The investigation involved the use of sophisticated covert techniques. The investigators had trespassed on land, installed tiny remote surveillance equipment, and hid in bushes in camouflage outfits in order to film the South Dorset Hunt and its staff on numerous occasions.

It transpired that the League Against Cruel Sports viewed all of the evidence obtained in this way, retaining all original copies of filmed material, and passed on copies of excerpts deemed relevant to the police. The Crown Prosecution Service brought a case against the defendant without ever having sight of all the material obtained by the League Against Cruel Sports.

What made this arrangement particularly concerning to the defence was that, at the time of the investigation, the police, the Crown Prosecution Service and the League Against Cruel Sports were all members of an organisation called PAW or the Partnership for Action Against Wildlife Crime. This organisation is a multi-agency body, set up by DEFRA, and comprises representatives of the organisations involved in wildlife enforcement in the United Kingdom. PAW has a memorandum of understanding designed to ensure that police wildlife officers throughout the country are supported by all partner organisations. Training courses involving the investigation of wildlife offences were run by the police for partner organisations including the League Against Cruel Sports and by organisations such as the League Against Cruel Sports for the police.

Despite the close cooperation between the police and the League as a result of this arrangement, no consideration had been given by the police to authorising the covert surveillance being undertaken by the League. The Regulation of Investigatory Powers Act 2000 provides the statutory framework for the authorisation of covert surveillance in England and Wales. Part II of the Act deals with surveillance. Section 27 provides that conduct to which Part II applies, including directed and intrusive covert surveillance,[11] is lawful *if* it has been authorised under the provisions of the Act. It was accepted in the *Leadbetter* case that no consideration had been given to whether the covert surveillance undertaken by the League could or should have been authorised by the police. During an abuse of

---

[10] *R v Christopher Leadbetter*, 21 January 2010.

[11] For the definitions of 'directed' and 'intrusive' surveillance, see s 26.

process argument heard at a pre-trial hearing in the case, the Crown Prosecution Service accepted that the Regulation of Investigatory Powers Act 2000 applied to the League's investigation. The district judge hearing the case held that the Regulation of Investigatory Powers Act 2000 applied to the investigation and accepted that no authority had been obtained. He left it to the trial judge to consider whether the evidence obtained as a result of the unauthorised investigation should be excluded under Police and Criminal Evidence Act 1984, s 78.

As a result of the issues raised in the case, the Crown Prosecution Service amended its guidance on the HA 2004 to include consideration of the Regulation of Investigatory Powers Act 2000 point.[12] The guidance accepts that non-governmental organisations such as the League often conduct surveillance of hunting meetings and other rural activities. The guidance maintains that no authorisation needs to be sought where a non-governmental organisation conducts the surveillance for its own purposes. In circumstances where the police are aware of the intention of an non-governmental organisations to conduct covert surveillance and intend making use of the surveillance product in the event that it reveals evidence of a crime, the guidance now recommends that it would be appropriate to seek authorisation. The guidance states that this would undoubtedly be the case where the non-governmental organisation is tasked to conduct the surveillance, whether explicitly or by necessary implication. The guidance suggests that no authorisation would be required where the police neither initiate nor encourage the surveillance, although it is difficult to envisage such a scenario given the close working relationship between the police and their partner organisations in PAW.

While the guidance will be of assistance to courts determining whether a breach of the Police and Criminal Evidence Act 1984 should mean that the product of unauthorised covert surveillance is excluded from a particular case, that will remain a matter to be determined on the facts of an individual case. It will be interesting, however, to see how many legal challenges arise as a result of the partnership between the police and non-governmental organisations which both campaign for changes to wildlife crime legislation and involve themselves in the investigation and prosecution of wildlife offences.

At the time of writing, the future of this most controversial piece of legislation is unclear. The Association of Chief Police Officers has announced that HA 2004 offences are not a policing priority, and the Conservative Party has promised a free vote on the issue of repeal of the

---

[12]   The Crown Prosecution Service Guidance on the Hunting Act 2004, as updated 14 January 2010, available at www.cps.gov.uk/legal/h_to_k/hunting_act/.

HA 2004. Whatever the future of the Act, in the short time that it has been on the statute books it has provided some excellent sport to those who ride to hounds in the criminal courts.

8.21 Summary

- Hunting is currently regulated by the provisions of the HA 2004.

- The Act creates two distinct forms of hunting: unlawful hunting and lawful exempt hunting.

- A person commits an offence if he hunts a wild mammal with a dog unless his hunting is exempt.

- Searching for a mammal is not an unlawful act. The offence is committed when an identifiable mammal has been actively and intentionally pursued.

- Once the defence of exempt hunting has been raised, either by the defendant or on the facts of the case, it is for the prosecution to prove, to the criminal standard, that the defendant's hunting was outside the requirements of the relevant exemption.

9   Badgers

9.1   Introduction

It may seem strange that a chapter in a book about field sports is devoted to badgers. One of the reasons is that, due to the extraordinary level of protection afforded to this creature, a large number of people associated with field sports have fallen foul of the laws protecting badgers.

When one considers that this is a mammal that is not endangered, may be largely responsible for the spread of bovine tuberculosis and, despite Kenneth Graeme's best efforts to portray it as a wise and kindly creature, is a pugnacious predator, it is also remarkable that it is an animal that has been singled out for such extreme legal protection.

9.2   Protection of Badgers Act 1992

The different pieces of legislation that have historically provided protection for badgers have been mostly amalgamated into the PBA 1992. The Act is titled 'An Act to consolidate the Badgers Act 1973, the Badgers Act 1991 and the Badgers (Further Protection) Act 1991'. Section 1 creates an offence if a person, except as permitted by the Act, wilfully kills, takes or injures a badger or attempts to kill, take or injure a badger.

Section 1(2) then apparently partially reverses the burden of proof in relation to an attempt to kill, take or injure a badger. The section states that:

> (2) If, in any proceedings for an offence under subsection (1) above consisting of attempting to kill, injure or take a badger, there is evidence from which it could reasonably be concluded that at the material time the accused was attempting to kill, injure or take a badger, he shall be presumed to have been attempting to kill, injure or take a badger unless the contrary is shown.

It is interesting, following the case of *Scott, Heard and Summersgill*,[1] to consider whether this partial reverse burden would stand up to the reasoning applied to the attempt to reverse the burden in the HA 2004.

---

[1]   *DPP v Wright* and *R on the application of Scott, Heard and Summersgill v Taunton Deane Magistrates' Court* [2009] EWHC 105 (Admin), 2009 WL 289265.

The reason that it would appear that s 1(2) only partially reverses the burden is that it only specifies that a presumption exists until the contrary is shown. The section does not specify that it is for the defendant to provide evidence to show that the contrary is true, and it is not difficult to conceive of a situation where the answers given in cross examination could show that such a presumption is unsustainable. It is also hard to conceive of the necessity for such a presumption. No such presumption is made where a person is accused of actually killing, taking or injuring a badger. The fact that the section stipulates that the presumption arises in proceedings where it could be reasonably concluded that the accused was attempting to kill, injure or take a badger raises another fascinating question. It would appear on any proper interpretation of criminal jurisprudence that the only time it is reasonable to conclude that an accused has committed an offence is at the point that a verdict is passed down. At this point any presumption is clearly unnecessary.

Section 1(3) creates an offence if:

> (3) A person ..., except as permitted by or under this Act, [he] has in his possession or under his control any dead badger or any part of, or anything derived from, a dead badger.

Section 1(4) goes on to provide a statutory defence in that:

> (4) A person is not guilty of an offence under subsection (3) above if he shows that—
>
> (a) the badger had not been killed, or had been killed otherwise than in contravention of the provisions of this Act or of the Badgers Act 1973; or
>
> (b) the badger or other thing in his possession or control had been sold (whether to him or any other person) and, at the time of the purchase, the purchaser had had no reason to believe that the badger had been killed in contravention of any of those provisions.

The effect of these two sections would appear to be that a man given a badger hair shaving brush by his aunt for Christmas would have to prove, should he be prosecuted, that, at the time she bought the brush, his aunt had had no reason to believe that the badger had been killed unlawfully. The old standard response that no prosecutor would bring such a case did not persuade the court considering the reverse burden in relation to the HA 2004 and may not provide a full answer in regard to these two sections.

Section 1(5) provides a power to the owners and occupiers of land, their servants and the police to require the name and address of anyone found committing an offence, and a power to require that the offender leave the land on which the offence was committed. A failure to leave or provide the relevant details is also an offence.

Section 2 of the Act is headed 'Cruelty' and makes it an offence if a person:

    (a) ... cruelly ill-treats a badger;

    (b) ... uses any badger tongs in the course of killing or taking, or attempting to kill or take, a badger;

    (c) except as permitted by or under this Act, digs for a badger; or

    (d) ... uses for the purpose of killing or taking a badger any firearm other than a smooth bore weapon of not less than 20 bore or a rifle using ammunition having a muzzle energy not less than 160 foot pounds and a bullet weighing not less than 38 grains.

Section 2(2) also provides a similar partial reverse burden to the one discussed above in relation to an attempt to take, kill or injure a badger.

Section 3 provides a series of protections to a badger's sett. Section 3 states that:

A person is guilty of an offence if, except as permitted by or under this Act, he interferes with a badger sett by doing any of the following things—

    (a) damaging a badger sett or any part of it;

    (b) destroying a badger sett;

    (c) obstructing access to, or any entrance of, a badger sett;

    (d) causing a dog to enter a badger sett; or

    (e) disturbing a badger when it is occupying a badger sett,

intending to do any of those things or being reckless as to whether his actions would have any of those consequences.

Section 14 of the Act provides a definition for a sett which is 'any structure or place which displays signs indicating current use by a badger'.

9.3   The Green case

The significance of this definition was explored in the case of *CPS v Green*.[2] This case was an appeal by way of case stated to the divisional court following the acquittal of four men charged with offences under s 3(a) of the Act, one of the defendants having also been charged and

---

2   [2001] 1 WLR 505.

acquitted of an offence under s 3(d). The brief facts of the case are that the four defendants had inadvertently trespassed on land belonging to the Ribley Estate in Lincolnshire, having been given permission to be on an adjoining estate for the purpose of vermin control. Two of the defendants were seen digging in the vicinity of a badger sett. The holes that were dug were alleged to have been above the tunnels that formed part of the sett, the defendants having introduced a ferret into a hole in the vicinity of the sett.

The sett in question was complex, allegedly consisting of a series of underground tunnels and at least 10 holes. Although the sett was not registered with English Nature, all parties agreed that a number of the holes could be said to be part of an active sett. The prosecution case was that all of the holes, and the area above the tunnels that they claimed linked the holes were to be considered part of the sett. The prosecution therefore made their case on the basis that digging into the ground within the area that the holes surrounded equated to interfering with a sett.

The activity of the defendants took place inside an isosceles triangle created by three holes. The first two holes, one and two, were about 50 to 60 yards apart. A further hole, hole 9, was about 50 to 60 yards to the west of a direct line between hole 1, to the south, and hole 2 to the north.

The prosecution claimed that the defendants had introduced a terrier into hole one with a radio locator on its collar, with a view to locating a badger. The defence case was that a ferret was introduced into the hole in order to locate a rabbit.

The court of first instance found no evidence to suggest that a terrier was introduced into the sett, the prosecution having relied upon an unevidenced contention that this must have been the case. The court then went on to consider whether the digging, which had been witnessed, amounted to interference with a sett.

The stipendiary magistrate found that there was no evidence that hole 1 actually connected, by way of tunnels, to the rest of the sett. He also found that there was no evidence that hole 1 was currently being used by badgers. In his judgment he stated that:

> I found it was very likely there was a pattern of tunnels under ground which would not be reflected in any way by what might be seen on the surface by way of holes. The pattern of tunnels would come within the definition of badger sett.

I found, therefore, that the Respondents had dug down over a relatively small area to a maximum of two feet in the vicinity of the badger sett. They had back filled what they had dug. I concluded that there was no evidence that the Respondents had broken into the tunnel system.

He went on to find that, as there was no evidence that the structure of the tunnels that did form part of an active sett had been damaged, it was not possible to find the defendants guilty.

The divisional court was asked two questions:

Whether the stipendiary magistrate was entitled, on the basis of the evidence which was properly adduced before him, to conclude that the badger sett did not include the area up to and including the surface area above the system of tunnels and chambers given the statutory definition of a badger sett.

If the answer to the first question is 'no', whether the stipendiary magistrate was entitled, on the basis of the evidence properly adduced before him, to conclude that the actions of the respondents in digging into the surface area did not amount to interference with the sett by damaging it.

Roch LJ and Wright J heard the case. Roch LJ gave the judgment of the court and decided that Parliament's intention, in defining a badger sett in s 14, was to ensure that the terms of the Act did not apply to tunnels and chambers constructed by badgers which were no longer in current use.

The court also found that it could not have been Parliament's intention that a person walking in the country who walks over a badger sett, intending or being reckless as to whether he disturbs the badger inside, would be committing an offence. Roch LJ stated that:

The meaning given to the phrase 'badger sett' should be clear and should also be confined. In my judgment, the phrase 'badger sett' refers to the tunnels and chambers constructed by badgers and the entrance holes to those tunnels and chambers. It may apply to other structures; where badgers, for example, occupy culverts or disused sheds for their shelter or refuge.

Roch LJ went on to say that the definition that the appellants had proposed, which included the complete area in which a sett was located, including the land over that lay on top of the network of tunnels, would place people like farmers in far too difficult a position and would make the law imprecise.

Roch LJ also observed that, had the prosecution charged the defendants with an offence under s 2(1) of digging for a badger, then the burden of proof would have been reversed and the court could have decided on the case that the prosecution were really seeking to make. Roch LJ determined that it was not necessary to stretch the meaning of 'badger sett' in order to provide protection to badgers against the activity that the prosecution alleged that the defendants were engaged in.

9.4   Overview of Green

Two important principles emerge from *Green*. The first is that the prosecution must show that a defendant was interfering with the actual tunnel network in order to achieve a conviction under s 3. The second is that it is not enough to show that one hole in the ground is an active badger sett, with evidence of current occupation, and invite the court to find on that basis that every other hole in a particular location is part of an active sett. The prosecution must show that the hole that a defendant is alleged to have interfered with shows signs of current use, or that the tunnel connected to that hole forms part of the network of tunnels that a badger is currently occupying. It is not possible for the court to make that assumption without the benefit of positive evidence. While the prosecution is likely to argue that to obtain such evidence would require it to interfere with a badger sett in a way that is undesirable, a court cannot be sure that a defendant was interfering with an active sett in the absence of such positive evidence.

9.5   Protection of Badgers Act 1992, continued

Section 4 of the Act creates an offence of selling or offering a live badger for sale. Section 5 makes it an offence to ring, tag or otherwise mark a badger without having obtained a licence.

Section 6 contains a number of statutory defences. The section states that:

> A person is not guilty of an offence under this Act by reason only of—
>
> (a) taking or attempting to take a badger which has been disabled otherwise than by his [unlawful] act and is taken or to be taken solely for the purpose of tending it [and releasing it when no longer disabled];
>
> (b) killing or attempting to kill a badger which appears to be so seriously injured or in such a condition that to kill it would be an act of mercy [has been so seriously disabled otherwise than by his unlawful act that there was no reasonable chance of it recovering];
>
> (c) unavoidably killing or injuring a badger as an incidental result of a lawful action;
>
> (d) doing anything which is authorised under the Animals (Scientific Procedures) Act 1986.

Section 7 provides a further statutory defence to a person accused of killing or taking, or attempting to kill or take, or injuring a badger in the course of attempting to kill or take it, where the reason for his actions is preventing serious damage to land, crops, poultry or any other form of property. A defendant will not be entitled to the benefit of this defence if it had become apparent before he took action that such action would be necessary and he had not applied for a licence under s 10 as soon as reasonably practicable, or his application for a licence had not been determined. What this means in practice is that either a person must hold a licence to benefit from this defence or he must catch the badger in the act of damaging the property that he seeks to protect.

Section 8 creates statutory defences to s 3 offences of interfering with badger setts. The first defence mirrors the defence set out in s 7 above, and includes the requirement to hold a licence. A further defence is contained in s 8(3) that enables a defendant to plead that the interference was incidental to a lawful operation that he was undertaking and could not reasonably have been avoided. This defence protects a range of individuals including, for example, those building a new road who come across a badger sett that they had not known existed in the course of their excavations.

Section 9 provides a statutory defence in relation to the possession of live badgers to those who possess a badger in the course of their business as carriers. It also provides a defence to a person possessing a live badger that has been disabled, not by an unlawful act of that person, where it is necessary for the badger to remain with that person while he tends it and until her releases it back into the wild.

Section 10 creates a series of licenses. The requirements and extent of the licenses are set out in the Act. For the purposes of this book it is unnecessary to examine the provisions of s 10 in detail due to the fact that so few licences have ever been issued to anyone who is not a vet, a scientist researching badgers or a government employee. The number of licenses issued to kill badgers for the protection of livestock remains academically small.

Section 11 provides a series of powers to the police for the enforcement of the provisions of the Act. These powers include the power to stop and search individuals and vehicles without warrant; the power, under warrant, to enter land and seize equipment and other items; and the power of arrest.

Section 11A makes it an offence to attempt to commit any of the offences set out in the Act or to possess any equipment for the purpose of committing an offence under the Act.

Section 12 determines the penalties for the offences created by the Act and allows for forfeiture of badger skins seized following the commission of an offence and weapons and other items used in the commission of an offence. Most offences created by the Act are summary offences. The cruelty offences contained within s 2(1)(a) to (c), the offence of introducing a dog into a badger sett contained within s 3(d), and the offence of selling a live badger contained at s 4 are all either way offences attracting a sentence of not more than 3 years in the Crown Court.

Section 12ZA extends the time limit for bringing prosecutions under the Act to 6 months from the time that a prosecutor was in possession of sufficient evidence to warrant bringing a prosecution. The section only allows the time limits to be extended to a maximum of 2 years from the date of the commission of an offence. The section also provides that a certificate by the prosecutor of the date on which he was in possession of sufficient evidence to bring proceedings shall be conclusive evidence of the fact of that date.

Section 13 relates to the powers of the court in the event that a dog has been used in the commission of an offence under the Act. This section allows the court to order the destruction or disposal of a dog used in the commission of an offence and the disqualification from owning or keeping a dog of a person convicted of an offence. The section also gives the court powers to order that a person convicted under the Act should pay the reasonable expenses associated with the disposal or destruction of the dog used by them in the commission of an offence. There are statutory provisions for appealing against orders made under this section.

9.6 Overview

When the Badger Bill was passing through the Lords, Lord Mancroft stated that:

> I hope that this important piece of legislation ... will have removed badgers from the political arena for some time to come. I believe that they will then be the most protected animal in Europe, if not the world. This is quite right because they are subjected in some areas and at times to a type of cruelty which is not directed at any other animal. So it is right that we should give them this extra protection.[3]

Lord Mancroft's reasoning is worth considering as it appears attractive at first glance and provides a measure of justification for the extreme protections and sanctions contained within the Act. It is the sort of reasoning that would appear uncontroversial if it were applied to humans that had suffered extreme ill treatment historically. What may be harder to understand is how the concept of compensating a particular species of animal is justifiable. If badgers have been particularly badly

---

[3] See *Hansard*, HL Deb, vol 530, col 760, 27 June 1991.

treated, it is clearly appropriate that the law should prevent such excesses. It is much harder to argue that because of past excesses, badgers should receive a level of protection that goes far beyond that which is necessary to prevent the ill treatment of other wild animals. It remains to be seen, in the light of the devastating effect of bovine tuberculosis on the livestock industry, whether the protections afforded by the Act will remain unchallenged in the future.

9.7   Summary

- Badgers and their habitat benefit from a higher level of protection than almost any other animal in the United Kingdom.

- It is an offence to intentionally kill, take or injure a badger, or attempt to do so.

- It is also an offence to interfere with a badger sett, either intentionally or recklessly.

- The burden of proof in relation to some badger-related offences is partially reversed.

- It is for the prosecution to prove that the individual hole in the ground on which a prosecution is based was an active badger sett at the time of the allegations against the defendant.

- In cases involving allegations of interference with badger setts, it must be proved that the defendant interfered with the actual tunnel network of an active sett, rather than merely disturbing the soil above an active sett.

10 Deer

10.1 Introduction

Deer, being the largest wild mammals in England and Wales, and as a result of being highly prized for their venison, have always occupied a special place in hierarchy of hunted game. Historically, deer could only be hunted by the King and his courtiers, and the penalties for taking the King's deer were extremely severe.

Deer are protected from poaching by the provisions of the DA 1991. Prior to the HA 2004 coming into force, the wild deer population in England and Wales was controlled by a combination of stalking and hunting. At the time of the hunting ban three staghound packs hunted regularly in the West Country: the Quantock, the Devon and Somerset and the Tiverton. In addition, the New Forest Buckhounds hunted in Hampshire.

Hunting deer on Exmoor and the Quantocks was historically a very effective method of controlling and conserving the population for a number of reasons. First, a large number of farmers work the land in that area. The hunts were run by farmers for farmers, and ensured a general level of consensus and cooperation as to the appropriate size of population that could be sustained by the region. Second, the hunts were able to ensure that the weaker and less healthy deer were selectively culled. This ensured the survival of the fittest and best deer within the herds.

Although it is generally agreed to be very important to sustain herds of deer in the West Country, as part of the biodiversity of the region and due in no small part to the contribution that deer make to tourism, an adult deer can eat as much in the way of crops, grass or any other naturally occuring foodstuff as three adult sheep over an equivalent period of time. As a result, following the hunting ban there has been a greater call for deer to be culled by stalking.

The law as it relates to shooting deer takes into account the different species of deer that live wild in England and Wales, their breeding seasons and their size.

10.2   Poaching deer

DA 1991, s 1 creates two offences related to the poaching of deer.

Section 1(1) makes it an offence if:

> (1) … any person enters any land without the consent of the owner or occupier or other lawful authority in search or pursuit of any deer with the intention of taking, killing or injuring it, …

Section 1(2) creates a further offence if any person, while on any land:

> (a) intentionally takes, kills or injures, or attempts to take, kill or injure, any deer,
>
> (b) searches for or pursues any deer with the intention of taking, killing or injuring it, or
>
> (c) removes the carcase of any deer,
>
> without the consent of the owner or occupier of the land or other lawful authority.

Both offences are subject to a statutory defence contained within s 1(3), which provides that a person shall not be found guilty of an offence under s 1(1) or (2) by reason of anything done in the belief that:

> (a) he would have the consent of the owner or occupier of the land if the owner or occupier knew of his doing it and the circumstances of it; or
>
> (b) he has other lawful authority to do it.

In common with other poaching statutes, in s 1(4) the Act also provides authorised persons with a power to require those who they reasonably suspect of committing an offence under s 1(1) or (2) to provide their full names and addresses and to leave the land immediately.

An authorised person for the purposes of s 1(4) is, 'the owner or occupier of the land or any person authorised by the owner or occupier, and includes any person having the right to take or kill deer on the land'.

10.3   Legal framework relating to the control of deer

The DA 1991 prescribes the closed seasons during which deer must not be taken. Schedule 1 to the Act, which contains the closed seasons, is set out at Appendix B4. It is worth noting that there is no closed season in relation to muntjac. Section 2 makes it an offence for a person to intentionally kill a deer of a species set out in Sch 1 during a closed season. Section 2(3) provides a statutory defence in relation to farmed deer.

Section 3 also makes it an offence to kill deer following the first hour after sunset and before the beginning of the first hour after sunrise.

Section 4 deals with the weapons that are prohibited in relation to killing deer. Section 4(1) creates an offence if any person:

(a) sets in position any article which is a trap, snare, or poisoned or stupefying bait and is of such a nature and so placed as to be calculated to cause bodily injury to any deer coming in contact with it, or

(b) uses for the purpose of taking or killing any deer any trap, snare or poisoned or stupefying bait, or any net,

Section 4(2) also makes it an offence if any person:

(2) ... for the purpose of taking or killing or injuring any deer—

(a) any firearm or ammunition mentioned in Schedule 2 to this Act,

(b) any arrow, spear or similar missile, or

(c) any missile, whether discharged from a firearm or otherwise, carrying or containing any poison, stupefying drug or muscle-relaxing agent, ...

Schedule 2 to the Act, which contains details of the prohibited firearms and ammunition, is set out at Appendix B5.

Section 6 sets out a number of statutory defences to charges brought under s 2, s 3 or s 4, including that an injured or diseased deer was killed in order to prevent it from suffering, and that a dependant juvenile deer was or was likely to be deprived of its mother.

Section 7 creates a number of statutory defences relating to occupiers of land.

Section 7(1) provides a defence to an occupier of land who kills a deer during a closed season if the deer was killed on cultivated land, pasture or enclosed woodland. Section 7(2) allows an occupier to use a smooth bore gun:

(2) ... of not less gauge than 12 bore which is loaded with—

(a) a cartridge containing a single non-spherical projectile weighing not less than 22.68 grammes (350 grains); or

(b) a cartridge purporting to contain shot each of which is .203 inches (5.16 millimetres) in diameter (that is to say, size AAA).

Section 7(3) requires a person seeking to benefit from the defences set out in s 7(1) and (2) to show that:

(a) he had reasonable grounds for believing that deer of the same species were causing, or had caused, damage to crops, vegetables, fruit, growing timber or any other form of property on the land;

(b) it was likely that further damage would be so caused and any such damage was likely to be serious; and

(c) his action was necessary for the purpose of preventing any such damage.

Section 8 creates a system of licensing, exempting individuals from certain provisions of ss 2 to 4 when they are in possession of a licence issued by Natural England, in relation to land in England, or the Welsh Ministers in relation to land in Wales.

Section 8(3) allows for the licensing of the use of any net, trap, stupefying drug or muscle-relaxing agent of a type authorised by the licence; and the use of any missile carrying or containing such stupefying drug or muscle-relaxing agent and the discharging of any such missile by any means authorised by the licence. Section 3B requires that such a licence is issued only on the grounds of preserving public health or safety, or for conserving the natural heritage.

10.4   Summary

- The DA 1991 creates the legal framework realting to the control of deer.

- Section 1 creates two offences of poaching deer.

- Schedule 1 defines the closed season for killing deer and creates a series of offences relating to the timing and weapons used for killing deer.

11 A Brief Overview of the Law Relating to Guns

11.1 Introduction

Firearms legislation in England and Wales is well covered in other texts and too broad a subject to be dealt with in depth here. A brief consideration of the statutory framework relating to gun ownership and use will hopefully be of assistance to readers.

The most important piece of legislation in regard to firearms remains the Firearms Act 1968. The Act creates a requirement for all firearms, save for a number of specified exceptions, to be licensed. The Act creates two separate licensing regimes, one for shotguns and another for all other firearms.

Section 1 of the Act makes it an offence, subject to any exemption contained within the Act, for a person to possess, purchase or acquire a firearm without holding a firearms certificate that is in force at the time. It also creates an offence of possessing ammunition for a firearm to which s 1 applies without a current certificate, or possessing more ammunition than a current certificate allows.

Section 1(3) exempts shotguns and certain air weapons from the requirements of a firearms certificate. A shotgun is defined as a smooth-bore gun (not being an air gun), which has a barrel not less than 24 inches in length and no more than 2 inches in diameter, which either has no magazine or has a non-detachable magazine holding no more than two cartridges and is not a revolver gun.

Section 2 of the Act creates a parallel requirement to hold a shotgun certificate before possessing, purchasing or acquiring a shotgun. Section 4 makes it an offence to shorten the barrel of a shotgun to less than 24 inches, and makes it an offence to possess, purchase or acquire a shortened shotgun without holding a relevant firearms certificate.

Section 5 creates a general prohibition on private ownership of certain types of weapons, including almost all handguns and all automatic weapons. Possession of any of the weapons described by s 5 is an offence punishable by a statutory minimum period of imprisonment as set out in s 51(5) of 5 years for an offender aged 18 or over when he committed the offence, or 3 years for an offender who was under 18 at the time he committed the offence.

Sections 7 to 15 create a series of special exemptions from the requirement to hold firearms or shotgun certificates. These include exemptions for authorised firearms dealers, carriers and auctioneers and those employed to slaughter animals using a slaughtering instrument.

Section 19 creates an offence of carrying a firearm in a public place. The section holds that a person commits an offence if, without lawful authority or reasonable excuse, the proof of which lies on him, he has with him in a public place a loaded shotgun; an air weapon, whether loaded or not; or any other firearm together with ammunition suitable for that firearm or an imitation firearm. This offence does not relate to certification, and therefore possession of a current certificate does not provide a full defence.

11.2   Firearms and minors

Section 22 details the minimum ages for the lawful acquisition and possession of firearms. Section 22(1)(a) makes it an offence for a person under the age of 18 to purchase or hire an air weapon or ammunition. Section 22(1)(b) creates a similar offence for a person under 17 to purchase or hire a firearm or ammunition of any other description.

A person under the age of 14 is not permitted to be granted a firearm certificate. Section 22(2) makes it an offence for a person under 14 years of age to be in possession of any firearm or ammunition except in circumstances outlined in Firearms Act 1968, s 11(1) and (4) or Firearms (Amendment) Act 1988, s 15.

Firearms Act 1968, s 11(1) allows a person, including someone under 14, to carry firearm, under the instructions of a certificate holder, for the use of the certificate holder for sporting purposes. Section 11(4) allows a person, including a person under 14, to use an air weapon or miniature rifle, not exceeding 23 inch calibre, at a miniature rifle range or shooting gallery. Firearms (Amendment) Act 1988, s 15 allows members of approved rifle clubs, including those under 14, to possess a rifle and ammunition when engaged as a member of the club in connection with target shooting.

It is an offence for a person under the age of 15 to have with him an assembled shotgun except while under the supervision of a person over the age of 21, or while the shotgun is in a securely fastened gun cover so that it cannot be fired according to Firearms Act 1968, s 22(3).

Section 22(4) makes it an offence for a person under 18 to have with him an air weapon or ammunition for an air weapon, unless the provisions of section 23 are complied with. Section 23 allows a person under the age of 18 to have an air weapon with him under the supervision of a person over the age of 21. It also allows a person over 14 years old to have an air rifle and ammunition with him on private premises with the consent of the occupier.

In summary then the following applies:

- 18 years old – the minimum age for the purchase of air weapons and ammunition. Those under the age of 18 having air rifles must be supervised by a person over the age of 21 unless they are aged between 14 and 18, and are on private premises with the consent of the occupier.

- 17 years old – the minimum age for the purchase or hire of any other firearms or ammunition.

- 15 to 17 years old – a person between these ages may acquire a shotgun other than by hire or purchase, for example as a gift, as long as they hold a shotgun certificate.

- Under 15 years – must not have an assembled shotgun that is outside a securely fastened gun cover in their possession except under the supervision of someone over the age of 21.

- Under 14 years – must not acquire or possess any firearm, unless carrying it under instruction for sporting purposes, or whilst at a rifle club or miniature rifle range. Can only possess an air weapon under the supervision of a person over the age of 21.

- It is worth noting that, while a minor can use a shotgun under supervision by someone over the age of 21, unless the minor is in possession of a shotgun certificate there are only two ways he can lawfully be lent a shotgun. The first is by the occupier of private premises as long as the minor uses the shotgun on the premises and in the presence of the occupier. The second is at an approved clay pigeon event. There does not appear to be a lawful way for a parent to lend their shotgun to a minor who does not hold a certificate on land that the parent does not occupy, despite this appearing to be a fairly regular occurrence on private shoots.

11.3   Use of firearms by adults who do not hold certificates

With regard to shotguns, as stated above, a person may borrow a shotgun from the occupier of private premises for use on those premises and in the presence of the occupier, according to Firearms Act 1968, s11(5). A person may also use a shotgun at an approved clay pigeon event according to s 11(6).

The only other way that a person who does not hold a shotgun certificate can lawfully possess a shotgun is if one of the special exceptions to the need for a certificate contained within ss 7 to 15 apply.

In regard to firearms other than shotguns, Firearms (Amendment) Act 1988, s 16(1) allows a person over the age of 17, without holding a firearms certificate, to borrow a rifle from the occupier of private premises and use it on the premises in the presence of either the occupier or the servant of the occupier, as long as the occupier or servant in whose presence the rifle is used holds a current certificate and the use complies with any conditions on the certificate.

As stated above, Firearms (Amendment) Act 1988, s 15 allows members of approved rifle clubs, to possess a rifle and ammunition when engaged as a member of the club in connection with target shooting.

Again, the only other way that a person who does not hold a firearms certificate can lawfully possess a firearm is if one of the special exceptions to the need for a certificate contained within ss 7 to 15 apply.

11.4   Applications for and revocation of certificates

The grant of a certificate is ultimately a matter of discretion for the Chief Officer of Police in the local area. While the language of the Act appears to be mandatory, in that the Act states that a certificate *shall* be granted on the basis of the Chief Officer of Police satisfying himself of the criteria, the nature of the criteria the Chief Officer must be satisfied of provides a wide discretion.

The main difference between a firearms certificate and a shotgun certificate is that there is a requirement to provide a good reason for needing each individual firearm. When a person wishes to purchase a new firearm he must apply for a variation to his certificate, and be able to justify holding another firearm, whereas once a good reason has been provided for holding a shotgun certificate, the certificate permits the ownership of as many shotguns as can be safely accommodated and it is a much simpler process to add the details of individual shotguns held to the certificate.

With regard to firearms, before granting a certificate, Firearms Act 1968, s 27 requires a Chief Officer of Police to be satisfied:

(a) that the applicant is fit to be entrusted with a firearm to which section 1 of this Act applies and is not a person prohibited by the Act from possessing such a firearm;

(b) that he has a good reason for having in his possession, or for purchasing or acquiring, the firearm or ammunition in respect of which the application is made; and

(c) that in all the circumstances the applicant can be permitted to have the firearm or ammunition in his possession without danger to the public safety or to the peace.

In regard to shotguns, a Chief Officer of Police must be satisfied that the applicant can be permitted to possess a shotgun without danger to the public safety or to the peace. No certificate shall be granted or renewed if the Chief Officer of Police has reason to believe that the applicant is prohibited by the Act from possessing a shotgun or is satisfied that the applicant does not have a good reason for possessing, purchasing or acquiring one. Section 28(1A) provides that a good reason for possessing a shotgun includes that the gun is intended to be used for sporting or competition purposes or for shooting vermin. It also provides that an application shall not be refused merely because the applicant neither intends to use the gun himself nor to lend it to anyone else to use.

A firearms certificate can be revoked, according to s 30A, if a Chief Officer of Police has reason to believe:

(a) that the holder is of intemperate habits or unsound mind or is otherwise unfitted to be entrusted with a firearm; or

(b) that the holder can no longer be permitted to have the firearm or ammunition to which the certificate relates in his possession without danger to the public safety or to the peace.

The Chief Officer of Police may also partially revoke a firearms certificate if he believes that the holder of the certificate no longer has a good reason for possessing, purchasing or acquiring a particular firearm listed on the certificate.

A shotgun certificate can be revoked, according to s 30C, if the Chief Officer of Police is satisfied that the holder is prohibited by the Act from possessing a shotgun or cannot be permitted to possess a shotgun without danger to the public safety or peace.

11.5   Appeals

An appeal against a decision by a chief officer of police not to grant a certificate, or to revoke a certificate, lies, in England and Wales, to the Crown Court, according to s 44. As a result, it is a costly process for any person offended by the decision to undertake. The case of *Kavanagh*[1] provides that, as the Crown Court is fulfilling an administrative function in the course of such an appeal, it is not bound by the usual rules of civil or criminal evidence. Cusack J giving the first judgment, held that the Crown Court had to apply its discretion in the same way that the Chief Constable would have to apply his discretion when deciding on a licensing matter, and therefore was at liberty to take into account hearsay, unsupported by witness testimony, and decide the appropriate weight that such evidence should be given.

One of the main triggers for the use of the discretion not to grant, or to revoke a certificate, is a criminal conviction on the part of the applicant, or a person living in the same household as the applicant. The case of *Spencer-Stewart*[2] holds that the commission of offences that do not involve the slightest risk or likelihood of the use of a shotgun do not provide grounds for refusing or revoking certificates. Therefore an applicant's driving history should not provide grounds for suspecting that a danger to public safety or peace is inherent in the grant of a certificate.[3] It is worth noting that a combination of domestic violence and a history of driving with excess alcohol were not sufficient for a revocation to be upheld in the case of *Edwards*,[4] the certificate holder having shown a responsible attitude towards firearms and that he did not have a drink problem. In that case both the Crown Court and the High Court took the view that the domestic violence involved neither the threat nor the use of firearms.

As stated above, this is not the place for a full consideration of the case law and principles associated with the use of the discretion by firearms officers on behalf of the Chief Officers of Police. It is worth noting, however, that in practice, due to the nature of the discretion available to the police, the first piece of advice to any person with regard to certificates is to maintain a good relationship with their local firearms

---

[1]   *Kavanagh v Chief Constable of Devon and Cornwall* [1974] 2 WLR 762, [1974] QB 624.

[2]   *Spencer-Stewart v Chief Constable of Kent* (1989) 89 Cr App R 307.

[3]   See the Scottish case of *Luke v Little* 1980 SLT (Sh Ct) 138 for a further illustration of this principle.

[4]   *Chief Constable of Norfolk v Edwards* [1997] CLY 4151.

officer, and to ensure, as far as possible, that all reasonable advice and directions that the firearms officer gives are followed. This is generally a more effective approach than a lengthy considerations of the academic legal position that an applicant may find himself or herself in.

11.6 Miscellaneous considerations

There are three offences, in regard to firearms, that are worthy of a brief consideration in the context of field sports: discharging a firearm within 50 feet of the centre of the highway, trespassing with a firearm and being drunk in possession of a loaded gun.

Highways Act 1980, s 161(2)(b) makes it an offence to discharge a firearm within 50 feet of the centre of a highway, without lawful authority or excuse, in consequence of which a user of the highway is injured, interrupted or endangered. The penalty for committing such an offence is a fine not exceeding level 3. The offence does not apply to footpaths and bridleways.

Despite the clear wording of the section, there appears to be a general misconception that discharging a firearm near a highway, footpath or bridleway is by its very nature an unlawful act. As stated above, Firearms Act 1968, s 19 makes carrying a firearm in a public place unlawful without reasonable excuse in most circumstances. There are clear codes of practice that ought to be followed in relation to the use of firearms to ensure that no one's safety is endangered by the discharge of a firearm. Despite these considerations, discharging a firearm with the appropriate reasons and permissions near a highway or other right of way is not an offence unless the requirements of s 161 are made out.

Firearms Act 1968, s 20(2) makes it an offence without reasonable excuse for a person to enter any land as a trespasser while he has a firearm in his possession. The case of *Christopher Brannan*[5] holds that the offence is committed even if the firearm is an air rifle. The importance of this offence is that it underlies the principle in relation to all field sports that the permission of a land owner or occupier is an essential ingredient in the lawful enjoyment of any field sport. In those situations where there is a disagreement between neighbours regarding shooting, this offence is a potential hazard.

Licensing Act 1872, s 12 still provides an offence of being drunk in possession of any loaded firearms, the maximum sentence for which is a penalty not exceeding level 1 or imprisonment of one month. It is worth

---

[5]   *Brannan (Christopher)* 1994 SLT 728.

noting that the offence is only made out if a person can be shown to be drunk, and the blood alcohol level of an individual will not be probative of this unless his behaviour and general appearance of intoxication can also be established.

11.7   Summary

- The Firearms Act 1968 still provides the basic legislative framework for gun ownership in England and Wales.

- Virtually all firearms, save for most air weapons, require certification to be lawfully possessed, purchased or acquired.

- The process of obtaining a shotgun certificate is less onerous that the process for obtaining a firearms certificate, as each firearm needs to be individually justified by the certificate holder.

- The grant of a certificate and any subsequent revocation is a matter of police discretion. Any appeals against a refusal to grant or a decision to revoke must be heard in the Crown Court.

12 Animal Welfare and Expert Witnesses

12.1 Introduction

Having been confronted already by a chapter on badgers, readers may wonder why this work also contains a chapter on animal welfare. The reason is that both shooting and hunting involve the use of animals. Those who participate in field sports are likely to be owners and keepers of animals and many people concerned in field sports are also livestock keepers. Due to the way in which animal rights organisations currently operate, a keeper of animals who also engages in or supports field sports may find themselves targeted with regard to an animal welfare investigation or prosecution. As a result, it was considered that a general overview of the law as it currently relates to the promotion of animal welfare may be of assistance.

Most criminal cases involving an allegation of a failure with regard to animal welfare have something in common with most HA 2004, PBA 1992 and poaching cases, ie the reliance on expert witness evidence in determining the issues. As a result, this chapter will also contain a brief consideration of the role of the expert witness in criminal proceedings.

It is worth noting that animal welfare legislation differs markedly in the manner in which it deals with wild animals as opposed to domestic animals, livestock and animals kept in captivity. 'Protected animals', as defined by Animal Welfare Act 2006 (AWA 2006), s 2, are animals that are:

(a) ... of a kind which is commonly domesticated in the British Islands

(b) ... under the control of man whether on a permanent or temporary basis, or

(c) ... not living in a wild state.

Such animals now receive a high level of welfare protection from the provisions of the Act.

While there are a number of pieces of legislation, such as the PBA 1992 and the WCA 1981 that criminalise specific acts with regard to wild mammals and birds, there is no general duty to ensure the welfare of wild animals imposed by law on landowners that is comparable with the duties imposed on the keepers of 'protected animals' by the AWA 2006.

The AWA 2006 replaced the old Protection of Animals Act 1911, which had provided the statutory basis for animal cruelty offences for nearly a century. The main change that the new Act brought in was to replace the old offence of animal cruelty with a new concept of a duty on a keeper of animals to ensure their welfare. It is easy to miss the significance of this change to animal keepers.

The offence of causing unnecessary suffering was contained within Protection of Animals Act 1911, s 1(1)(a), which provided:

> (1) If any person—
>
> > (a) shall ... by wantonly or unreasonably doing or omitting to do any act ... cause any unnecessary suffering ... to any animal ...
>
> such person shall be guilty of an offence of cruelty within the meaning of this Act ...

It was therefore necessary, before the AWA 2006 came into force, to show that an animal had suffered as a result of an act or omission on the part of the defendant. AWA 2006, s 9 now states:

> (1) A person commits an offence if he does not take such steps as are reasonable in all the circumstances to ensure that the needs of an animal for which he is responsible are met to the extent required by good practice.
>
> (2) For the purposes of this Act, an animal's needs shall be taken to include—
>
> > (a) its need for a suitable environment,
> >
> > (b) its need for a suitable diet,
> >
> > (c) its need to be able to exhibit normal behaviour patterns,
> >
> > (d) any need it has to be housed with, or apart from, other animals, and
> >
> > (e) its need to be protected from pain, suffering, injury and disease.

The obvious difference is that there is no longer any requirement for an animal to have actually suffered in order for an offence to have been committed. In practice, it is unlikely that prosecutions will succeed where no suffering is alleged, as it will be very difficult to prove that a healthy animal that has not experienced any suffering has not had its needs met. It is also worth noting that AWA 2006, s 4 retains the old offence of causing unnecessary suffering. Nonetheless, it is a radical step to criminalise the failure of an individual to discharge such loosely defined duties.

It is worth considering that, while the PBA 1992 prevents a landowner from killing, capturing or interfering with the home of a badger, there is no requirement to protect it from pain, suffering, injury or disease. As a result, the fact that a badger may be suffering from tuberculosis, leading to its slow, lingering death underground, will not cause the landowner whose land its sett is located on, to have any responsibility to alleviate its suffering. He will, however, have a statutory duty on him to protect his cattle from bovine tuberculosis, although it is unclear how he can discharge this duty given the strict provisions of the PBA 1992.

Similarly, while the Wild Mammals (Protection) Act 1996 provides in s 1 that:

> If, save as permitted by this Act, any person mutilates, kicks, beats, nails or otherwise impales, stabs, burns, stones, crushes, drowns, drags or asphyxiates any wild mammal with intent to inflict unnecessary suffering he shall be guilty of an offence.

There is no parallel duty on a landowner to control numbers of wild mammals in order to protect the welfare of other wild animals or birds on his property, or to prevent disease. In fact, despite the very clear science that demonstrates that predator control is an essential element of the protection of many species of birds and smaller woodland mammals, all current legislation aimed at wild animals deals only with prevention or regulation of the killing of wild animals rather than requiring culling on welfare grounds.

12.2   Animal Welfare Act 2006

As well as placing a new duty on the keepers of 'protected animals' to ensure that their needs are met, the AWA 2006 also created a series of new offences and provided some radical powers for those enforcing the Act.

One new offence that will undoubtedly be of interest to those engaged in field sports is contained within s 6. A person commits an offence under this section if he removes any part of a dog's tail, otherwise than for the purpose of its medical treatment, or he causes another person to do the same. A person also commits an offence if he is responsible for a dog and allows another person to remove the whole or part of a dog's tail, otherwise than for the purpose of its medical treatment or fails to take reasonable steps to prevent that happening.

The only way that a dog's tail can now be lawfully docked is if the dog is certified as a working dog by a vet and the docking takes place before it is 5 days old. It is a defence to an allegation of unlawful docking for a person to show that he reasonably believed the dog had been correctly certified as a working dog.

While the AWA 2006 provides significant new powers in relation to animals considered to be in distress, it is worth noting that these powers are only provided to local authority inspectors and police constables. Currently, there is an odd situation in regard to the policing of animal welfare offences, in that the RSPCA is responsible for a high proportion of the investigations and prosecutions currently brought under the Act but, despite intensive lobbying prior to the Act being passed, the RSPCA has not been given any statutory powers at all by the Act.

Section 18 provides that if a local authority inspector or police constable reasonably believes that a protected animal is suffering, he may take such steps as appear to him to be immediately necessary to alleviate the animals suffering. This includes a specific power under s 18(5) to take an animal into his possession if a vet certifies that the animal is suffering or that it is likely to suffer if its circumstances do not change. Once an animal has been confiscated under s 18(5) a magistrates' court may also order, under s 18(13) that any expenses incurred by anyone acting under the section shall be reimbursed by anyone it sees fit. In practical terms this means that, where an inspector or constable acts to confiscate an animal, the expenses associated with feeding and housing the animal can be ordered to be paid by the keeper, or anyone else the court deems responsible for the animal being confiscated. If a court does make such an order, the person against whom the order is made has the right of appeal to the Crown Court.

Section 19 provides a power of entry for a local authority inspector or police constable for the purpose of searching for a 'protected animal' and/or for the purpose of exercising a s 18 power, if he reasonably believes there is a protected animal on the premises and the animal is suffering or is likely to suffer. This power does not extend to any part of any premises that are used as a private dwelling. Entry into a premises used as a private dwelling must be under warrant, which can be issued according to s 19(4).

Section 20 further provides that a magistrates' court may order that an animal confiscated under s 18(5) can be treated, given into the possession of a specified person, sold, disposed of or destroyed. An application under s 20 can be made by the owner or any other person that the court considers has a sufficient interest in the animal.

The maximum penalty that a magistrates' court can impose for certain offences committed under the Act, including causing unnecessary suffering, is imprisonment for a term not exceeding 51 weeks or a fine not exceeding £20,000. In addition, the court can order that the defendant is deprived of ownership of the animal under s 33 and disqualified from owning, keeping or participating in keeping animals under s 34. A person who is disqualified may apply to the court for the termination of the order, but not before the end of a year from the date on which the order was made, or the end of any period specified by the court that made the order.

12.3   Unnecessary suffering

It is worth noting that the offence retained by s 4 of the Act relates to 'unnecessary suffering'. The case of *Isaac*[1] provides a helpful insight into the meaning of 'unnecessary suffering'. Holland J, quoting his own judgment in the unreported case of *R v Portsmouth Crown Court, ex parte Hall* states:

> ... the first issue for the Justices related to so much of the section as refers to 'unnecessary suffering', and raised for them at that stage the essential issue: was there evidence as to such element that a reasonable tribunal might convict on it?

> That basic question raised two particular questions for their consideration. First, was there enough evidence that this dog had suffered? If 'Yes', was there enough evidence that such suffering was unnecessary? As to the first of those two particular questions, I need say no more. As to the second, it is right to say more about the word 'unnecessary'. The drafting of this subsection, in my judgment, postulates that it may be inevitable, hence 'necessary', for an animal to experience suffering even when in the care of a reasonably competent, reasonably caring owner. When, however, the suffering is not inevitable, in that it can be terminated or alleviated by some reasonably practicable measure, then the suffering becomes unnecessary within the meaning of that subsection.

> Let it be assumed that both those issues were on the evidence to be resolved in favour of the prosecution. The second matter then raised for the Justices' consideration turned so much of the subsection as reads 'unreasonably doing or omitting to do any act.' In the particular circumstance of this case the information alleges an omission, and it is upon an omission that I focus attention.

> I would hold that in respect of this part of the subsection, again two questions are posed: (i) was there enough evidence that the Respondent had omitted to do anything so as to cause unnecessary suffering? (ii) if the answer were 'Yes', was there enough evidence that that omission was unreasonable; that is, viewed objectively, that no reasonably caring, reasonably competent owner would be guilty of a similar omission. I emphasise, the test is an objective one.' It is clear from this judgment that suffering is only 'unnecessary' if a

---

[1]   *Royal Society for the Prevention of Cruelty to Animals v Valerie Isaac* [1994] Crim LR 517.

reasonably caring and competent keeper of animals would have know, or ought to have known, that their actions or omissions would lead to suffering, and, despite this knowledge, continued to act or fail to act in a way that lead to suffering.

The case of *Peterssen v RSPCA*[2] provides further authority that the case law in regard to causing unnecessary suffering, dating back to the cases of *Barnard v Evans*[3] and *Greenwood v Backhouse*,[4] requires an element of guilty knowledge. As a result a person cannot be found guilty of causing unnecessary suffering unless it can be shown that he knew or ought to have known about the condition of the relevant animal.

It is also worth noting that the case of *R on the application of the RSPCA v C*[5] provides that, while the test for whether an animal was caused suffering is an objective test, a court is entitled to take all the circumstances of the case, including the youth of the defendant, into account, when determining whether their actions were reasonable. In that case the defendant was a 15-year-old girl who knew that her cat had an injured tail but was told by her father that the cat would not be taken to the vet unless its condition worsened. Her father pleaded guilty to causing unnecessary suffering but, despite his plea, the RSPCA decided to prosecute the daughter for an identical offence. The High Court found that the justices were right to find that in these circumstances, the daughter's failure to seek veterinary attention as a result of her father's instructions were reasonable in all the circumstances.

While it is clear that the s 4 offence requires guilty knowledge, it will be interesting to see if the s 9 offence of failing to meet the needs of a 'protected animal' is deemed to be a strict liability offence by the courts or whether that offence will also require a degree of *mens rea*.

12.4   Expert evidence

As stated above, most cases brought under the AWA 2006, the PBA 1992 or the HA 2004 will ultimately depend on expert opinion evidence for a successful conviction. It is easy to see why a court would require an expert to give evidence on whether signs of current activity have been produced by the prosecution to show that a hole in the ground is actually

---

[2]   [1993] Crim LR 852.

[3]   [1925] 2 KB 794.

[4]   (1902) 66 JP 519.

[5]   [2006] EWHC 1069 (Admin), (2006) 170 JP 463.

a badger sett. Similarly, it will almost always be necessary for a court to be provide with veterinary expert opinion on whether an animal is suffering from a disease process, the affects of which were avoidable.

Historically, expert evidence has not been dealt with in these cases as fastidiously as it ought to be in order to be of assistance to the court. It has not been unusual to see the prosecution in an animal welfare case provide a short statement from a vet stating that he or she has seen an animal and is of the view that it was suffering unnecessarily. This sort of baseless pronouncement is often confused with expert evidence, on the basis of it being an opinion that is held by an expert. The secret to dealing with expert evidence correctly, however, is in understanding that it is not what an expert thinks that is of assistance to a court, but why an expert thinks what he thinks, and whether his opinion can be safely justified on the basis of good science.

The case of *Regina v Turner (Terence)*[6] provides a good starting point for understanding when expert evidence is admissible and how it is likely to assist a court. In his judgment, Lawton LJ refers to Lord Mansfield's dicta in *Folkes v Chadd*:[7]

> the opinion of scientific men upon proven facts may be given by men of science within their own science. An expert's opinion is admissible to furnish the court with scientific information which is likely to be outside the experience and knowledge of a judge or jury. If on the proven facts a judge or jury can form their own conclusions without help, then the opinion of an expert is unnecessary. In such a case if it is given dressed up in scientific jargon it may make judgment more difficult. The fact that an expert witness has impressive scientific qualifications does not by that fact alone make his opinion on matters of human nature and behaviour within the limits of normality any more helpful than that of the jurors themselves; but there is a danger that they may think it does.

Lawton LJ went on to hold that a jury does not need an expert psychiatrist to tell them how ordinary people who are not suffering from mental illnesses are likely to react to the stresses and strains of life. The fact that an expert is willing to provide his opinion does not make it admissible as evidence.

As Lord Mansfield held, an expert's opinion is admissible in order to assist the court with those scientific truths that the court might otherwise fail to consider. As a result, it is essential for the prosecution to prove the

---

[6]   [1975] 2 WLR 56, [1975] QB 834.

[7]   (1782) 3 Doug KB 157.

facts on which expert opinion is based, rather than expecting a court to assume that an expert opinion is properly based. As Lawton LJ says in *Regina v Turner (Terence)*:[8]

> Before a court can assess the value of an opinion it must know the facts upon which it is based. If the expert has been misinformed about the facts or has taken irrelevant facts into consideration or has omitted to consider relevant ones, the opinion is likely to be valueless. In our judgment, counsel calling an expert should in examination in chief ask his witness to state the facts upon which his opinion is based. It is wrong to leave the other side to elicit the facts by cross-examination.

Criminal Procedure Rules 2005,[9] Part 33 deals with expert evidence in criminal proceedings. The guidelines contained in this part came about following a series of cases that considered the duty of experts and the contents of an expert's report.[10] Rule 33.2 sets out an expert's duty to the court by stating that:

(1) An expert must help the court to achieve the overriding objective by giving objective, unbiased opinion on matters within his expertise.

(2) This duty overrides any obligation to the person from whom he receives instructions or by whom he is paid.

(3) This duty includes an obligation to inform all parties and the court if the expert's opinion changes from that contained in a report served as evidence or given in a statement.

The case of *Liverpool Roman Catholic Archdiocesan Trustees Inc v Goldberg (No 3)*[11] provides judicial scrutiny of this duty. Evans-Lombe J considered the case of an expert who had a pre-exisiting relationship with one of the parties to an action. At para 11 he pointed out that:

> In his report, having described that relationship, Mr Flesch said: 'I do not believe that this [relationship] will affect my evidence: I certainly accept that it should not do so. But it is right that I should say that my personal sympathies are engaged to a greater degree than would probably be normal with an expert witness'.

It seems to me that this admission rendered Mr Flesch's evidence unacceptable as the evidence of an expert on grounds of the public policy that justice must be seen to be done as well as done. This is clear

---

[8] [1975] QB 834, 840.

[9] SI 2005/384.

[10] See Cresswell J, *National Justice Cia Naviera SA v Prudential Assurance Co Ltd (Ikerian Reefer)* [1993] 2 Lloyd's Rep 68, 81.

[11] [2001] 1 WLR 2337.

from the passage in the speech of Lord Wilberforce in *Whitehouse v Jordan*,[12] cited by Neuberger J, where Lord Wilberforce says:

> While some degree of consultation between experts and legal advisers is entirely proper, it is necessary that expert evidence presented to the court should be, *and should be seen to be*, the independent product of the expert, uninfluenced as to form or content by the exigencies of litigation. (emphasis added)

The role of an expert witness is special owing, as he does, duties to the court which he must discharge notwithstanding the interest of the party calling him, see per Evans-Lombe J in *Liverpool Roman Catholic Archdiocesan Trustees Inc v Goldberg (No 3)*:[13]

> I accept that neither section 3 of the 1972 Act nor the authorities under it expressly exclude the expert evidence of a friend of one or the parties. However, in my judgment, where it is demonstrated that there exists a relationship between the proposed expert and the party calling him which a reasonable observer might think was capable of affecting the views of the expert so as to make them unduly favourable to that party, his evidence should not be admitted however unbiased the conclusions of the expert might probably be. The question is one of fact, namely, the extent and nature of the relationship between the proposed witness and the party.

Rule 33.3 deals with the requirements of the contents of an expert's report and provides that:

(1) An expert's report must—

  (a) give details of the expert's qualifications, relevant experience and accreditation;

  (b) give details of any literature or other information which the expert has relied on in making the report;

  (c) contain a statement setting out the substance of all facts given to the expert which are material to the opinions expressed in the report, or upon which those opinions are based;

  (d) make clear which of the facts stated in the report are within the expert's own knowledge;

  (e) say who carried out any examination, measurement, test or experiment which the expert has used for the report and—

     (i) give the qualifications, relevant experience and accreditation of that person,

---

[12]   [1981] 1 WLR 246, 256–257.

[13]   [2001] 1 WLR 2337.

    (ii) say whether or not the examination, measurement, test or experiment was carried out under the expert's supervision, and

    (iii) summarise the findings on which the expert relies;

(f) where there is a range of opinion on the matters dealt with in the report—

    (i) summarise the range of opinion, and

    (ii) give reasons for his own opinion;

(g) if the expert is not able to give his opinion without qualification, state the qualification;

(h) contain a summary of the conclusions reached;

(i) contain a statement that the expert understands his duty to the court, and has complied and will continue to comply with that duty; and

(j) contain the same declaration of truth as a witness statement.

(2) Only sub-paragraphs (i) and (j) of rule 33.3(1) apply to a summary by an expert of his conclusions served in advance of that expert's report.

It is good practice to ensure that where either party intends to rely on expert evidence; both prosecution and defence experts provide fully compliant reports in advance of the trial. Clearly, the defence will not be in a position to know if they intend to rely on expert evidence until the prosecution have produced an initial expert report setting out the basis of any expert opinion that forms part of the case against the defendant. Criminal Justice Act 1988, s 30 makes expert reports admissible without the need for an expert to be called.

Rule 33.4 requires any party who wishes to rely on expert evidence to serve it on the court and the other party as soon as practicable and with any application in support. If either party so requires, they must be given an opportunity to inspect a record of any examination, measurement, test or experiment on which the expert's findings and opinions are based; and to inspect anything on which those examinations, measurements, tests or experiments were carried out.

Rule 33.6 makes provisions for expert meetings pre trial, With a view to narrowing the issues of expert agreement.

12.5 Summary

- The AWA 2006 creates a framework for the protection of domestic animals and animals under the control of man.

- The AWA 2006 creates a new duty on keepers of animals to ensure that the animal's needs are met, and creates an offence of failing to discharge the duty.

- The AWA 2006 retains the old offence of causing unnecessary suffering. The offence requires guilty knowledge on the part of the defendant, who is expected to do what a reasonably competent person would do in all the circumstances.

- The AWA 2006 provides new powers for local authority inspectors and police constables to enter premises and seize animals. The RSPCA has not been given these powers.

- Offences under the Act can attract fines of up to £20,000 and prison sentences of up to 51 weeks in the magistrates' court. In addition, the court can disqualify a defendant from keeping animals.

- The duties of expert witnesses and requirements regarding the contents of their reports are contained in Criminal Procedure Rules 2005, Part 33.

Appendices

Appendices

A1 Authority under Ground Game Act 1880, s 1

I [ ]¹

Of [ ] ²

In respect of the holding known as [ ]³ ('the land')

HMLR title number [ ]⁴

Confirm that [ ]⁵

Is:⁶

Resident in my household on the land

In my service or my employment on the land

Engaged to take ground game for reward

And I herby authorise him/her to take ground game (rabbits and hares) on the land⁷

With firearms⁸

At night⁹

Signed ....

Dated ....

---

[1] Insert full name.

[2] Insert full address.

[3] Insert sufficient description of holding.

[4] Insert title number if land registered and title number known.

[5] Insert name of person authorised.

[6] These categories are set out in GGA 1880, s 1(1)(b).

[7] Delete 1 or 2 as appropriate.

[8] See GGA 1880, s 1(1)(a).

[9] See explanation at para 5.3.

A2   Authority under Ground Game Act 1880, s 1[10]

I [ ][11]

Of [ ][12]

In respect of the holding known as [ ][13] ('the land')

HMLR title number [ ][14]

Confirm that [ ][15] is entitled to demand to see and inspect the written authority of any person found on the land to shoot, kill or take ground game on the land

Signed ....

Dated ....

Note. By virtue of the terms of the GGA 1880 any person if required by the bearer of this authority shall produce to the person so demanding the document by which he is authorised, and in default he shall not be deemed to be an authorised person.

---

[10] This authority allows the holder to inspect the authority to shoot ground game of others, see GGA 1880, s 1(1)(c).

[11] Insert full name.

[12] Insert full address.

[13] Insert sufficient description of holding.

[14] Insert title number if land registered and title number known.

[15] Insert name of person authorised.

A3   Appointment of deputation of a gamekeeper under Game Act 1831, ss 13, 14, 15 for use in England

This deed of appointment is made this day of 20[   ]

I,[16] of, lord of the manor of,[17] in the county of,[18] do pursuant to the Game Act 1831 hereby nominate, authorise, appoint and depute[19] of,[20] to be my gamekeeper of and within the manor of[21] *(or if appropriate and only part of the manor is being dealt with specify the part of the manor here)* ('the manor'), for as long as I shall not revoke this authority, with full power, licence and authority to kill any hare, pheasant, partridge rabbits or other game whatsoever, and wild fowl and fish, in and upon the manor, for my sole use and immediate benefit.

Signed as a deed

By [   ]

In the presence of

(Signed)

---

[16]   Insert first and second names.

[17]   Insert name of the manor.

[18]   Insert county.

[19]   Insert name of gamekeeper.

[20]   Insert address of gamekeeper.

[21]   Insert as footnote 17.

A4   Appointment of deputation of a gamekeeper under Game Act 1831, ss 13, 14, 15 for use in Wales

This deed of appointment is made this [ ] day of [ ] 20[ ]

I,[22] of, lord of the manor of,[23] in the county of,[24] do pursuant to the Game Act 1831 hereby nominate, authorise, appoint and depute[25] of,[26] to be my gamekeeper of and within the manor, lordship *or* royalty of in the County of [ ], in the principality of Wales[27] *(or if appropriate and only part of the manor is being dealt with specify the part of the manor here)* ('the manor'), for as long as I shall not revoke this authority, with full power, licence and authority to kill any hare, pheasant, partridge rabbits or other game whatsoever, and wild fowl and fish, in and upon the manor, for my sole use and immediate benefit.

Signed as a deed

By [ ]

In the presence of

(Signed)

---

[22]   Insert first and second names.

[23]   Insert name of the manor.

[24]   Insert county.

[25]   Insert name of gamekeeper.

[26]   Insert address of gamekeeper.

[27]   See GGA 1880, s 1(1)(a).

A5   Certificate of clerk of the Crown Court as to registration of gamekeeper

[Game Act 1831, ss 13, 14, 15]

I[28] clerk of the Crown Court for the area of [ ], for the purposes of the Game Act 1831 do hereby certify that[29] [ ] on the date of this certificate registered the appointment of[30] [ ] as a gamekeeper by[31] for the manor [*or* lands, *if in Wales*] of [ ].[32]

Dated, this [ ] day of [ ] ....

Signed ....

---

[28]   Insert name of clerk.

[29]   Insert name of the person registering the appointment.

[30]   Insert name of gamekeeper.

[31]   Insert name of lord of the manor.

[32]   Insert name of manor.

A6   Form of authorisation of person to shoot kill or take species permitted to be killed under a general or specific licence granted under Wildlife and Countryside Act 1981, s 16

I [ ]^{33} of [ ]^{34} confirm that [ ]^{35} is authorised by me to shoot, kill or take all species/the following species [ ]^{36} on my land known as [ ]^{37} permitted to be killed or taken by virtue of the general licence/a specific licence^{38} granted under Wildlife and Countryside Act 1981, s 16

Dated ....

Signed ....

---

[33] Insert full name of owner of land.

[34] Insert address of owner of land.

[35] Insert full name of person authorised.

[36] Delete as appropriate.

[37] Insert sufficient description of land.

[38] Delete as appropriate.

B1   Ground Game Act 1880[1]

An Act for the better protection of Occupiers of Land against injury to their Crops from Ground Game.

[7th September 1880]

1   Occupier to have a right inseparable from his occupation to kill ground game concurrently with any other person entitled to kill the same on land in his occupation

Every occupier of land shall have, as incident to and inseparable from his occupation of the land, the right to kill and take ground game thereon, concurrently with any other person who may be entitled to kill and take ground game on the same land: Provided that the right conferred on the occupier by this section shall be subject to the following limitations:

(1)   The occupier shall kill and take ground game only by himself or by persons duly authorised by him in writing:

    (a)   The occupier himself and one other person authorised in writing by such occupier shall be the only persons entitled under this Act to kill ground game with firearms;

    (b)   No person shall be authorised by the occupier to kill or take ground game, except members of his household resident on the land in his occupation, persons in his ordinary service on such land, and any one other person bona fide employed by him for reward in the taking and destruction of ground game;

    (c)   Every person so authorised by the occupier, on demand by any person having a concurrent right to take and kill the ground game on the land or any person authorised by him in writing to make such demand, shall produce to the person so demanding the document by which he is authorised, and in default he shall not be deemed to be an authorised person.

(2)   A person shall not be deemed to be an occupier of land for the purposes of this Act by reason of his having a right of common over such lands; or by reason of an occupation for the purpose of grazing or pasturage of sheep, cattle, or horses for not more than nine months.

---

[1]   As amended by all statutes and SIs up to the RRO 2007.

(3)   In the case of moorlands, and uninclosed lands (not being arable lands), the occupier and the persons authorised by him shall exercise the rights conferred by this section only from the eleventh day of December in one year until the thirty-first day of March in the next year, both inclusive; but this provision shall not apply to detached portions of moorlands or uninclosed lands adjoining arable lands, where such detached portions of moorlands or uninclosed lands are less than twenty-five acres in extent.

2   Occupier entitled to kill ground game on land in his occupation not to divest himself wholly of such right

Where the occupier of land is entitled otherwise than in pursuance of this Act to kill and take ground game thereon, if he shall give to any other person a title to kill and take such ground game, he shall nevertheless retain and have, as incident to and inseparable from such occupation, the same right to kill and take ground game as is declared by section one of this Act. Save as aforesaid, but subject as in section six hereafter mentioned, the occupier may exercise any other or more extensive right which he may possess in respect of ground game or other game, in the same manner and to the same extent as if this Act had not passed.

3   All agreements in contravention of right of occupier to destroy ground game void

Every agreement, condition, or arrangement which purports to divest or alienate the right of the occupier as declared, given, and reserved to him by this Act, or which gives to such occupier any advantage in consideration of his forbearing to exercise such right, or imposes upon him any disadvantage in consequence of his exercising such right, shall be void.

5   Saving clause

Where at the date of the passing of this Act the right to kill and take ground game on any land is vested by lease, contract of tenancy, or other contract bona fide made for valuable consideration in some person other than the occupier, the occupier shall not be entitled under this Act, until the determination of that contract, to kill and take ground game on such land. And in Scotland when the right to kill and take ground game is vested by operation of law or otherwise in some person other than the occupier, the occupier shall not be entitled by virtue of this Act to kill or take ground game during the currency of any lease or contract of tenancy under which he holds at the passing of this Act, or during the currency of any contract made bona fide for valuable consideration before the passing of this Act whereby any other person is entitled to take and kill ground game on the land.

6 Prohibition of Night Shooting, spring traps above ground or poison

Nothing in this Act shall affect any special right of killing or taking ground game to which any person other than the landlord, lessor, or occupier may have become entitled before the passing of this Act by virtue of any franchise, charter, or Act of Parliament.

7 As to non-occupier having right of killing game

Where a person who is not in occupation of land has the sole right of killing game thereon (with the exception of such right of killing and taking ground game as is by this Act conferred on the occupier as incident to and inseparable from his occupation), such person shall, for the purpose of any Act authorising the institution of legal proceedings by the owner of an exclusive right to game, have the same authority to institute such proceedings as if he were such exclusive owner, without prejudice nevertheless to the right of the occupier conferred by this Act.

8 Interpretation clause

For the purposes of this Act—

The words 'ground game' mean hares and rabbits.

9 Exemption from penalties

A person acting in accordance with this Act shall not thereby be subject to any proceedings or penalties in pursuance of any law or statute.

10 Saving of existing prohibitions

Nothing in this Act shall authorise the killing or taking of ground game on any days or seasons, or by any methods, prohibited by any Act of Parliament in force at the time of the passing of this Act.]

11 Short title

This Act may be cited for all purposes as the Ground Game Act, 1880.

B2 Game Act 1831[2]

2 What shall be deemed Game

The word 'game' shall for all the purposes of this Act be deemed to include hares, pheasants, partridges, grouse, heath or moor game, black game ...; and the words 'lord of a manor, lordship, or royalty, or reputed manor, lordship, or royalty,' shall throughout this Act be deemed to include a lady of the same respectively.

3 Days and Seasons during which Game shall not be killed. Penalty for laying poison to kill game

If any person whatsoever shall kill or take any game, or use any dog, gun, net, or other engine or instrument for the purpose of killing or taking any game, on a Sunday or Christmas Day, such person shall, on conviction thereof before two justices of the peace, forfeit and pay for every such offence such sum of money, not exceeding level 1 on the standard scale, as to the said justices shall seem meet, ...; and if any person whatsoever shall kill or take any partridge between the first day of February and the first day of September in any year, or any pheasant between the first day of February and the first day of October in any year, or any black game (except in the county of Somerset or Devon, or in the New forest in the county of Southampton,) between the tenth day of December in any year and the twentieth day of August in the succeeding year, or in the county of Somerset or Devon, or in the New forest aforesaid, between the tenth day of December in any year and the first day of September in the succeeding year, or any grouse commonly called red game between the tenth day of December in any year and the twelfth day of August in the succeeding year, or any bustard between the first day of March and the first day of September in any year, every such person shall, on conviction of any such offence before two justices of the peace, forfeit and pay for every head of game so killed or taken such sum of money, not exceeding level 1 on the standard scale], as to the said justices shall seem meet, and if any person, with intent to destroy or injure any game, shall at any time put or cause to be put any poison or poisonous ingredient on any ground, whether open or inclosed, where game usually resort, or in any highway, every such person shall, on conviction thereof before two justices of the

---

[2] This version should be as amended by all statutes and SIs up to the RRO 2007 if a section is missing it has been repealed.

peace, forfeit and pay such sum of money, not exceeding level 1 on the standard scale, as to the said justices shall seem meet, ...

3A   Sale of birds of game

If any person—

(a)   sells or offers or exposes for sale, or

(b)   has in his possession or transports for the purposes of sale,

any bird of game to which this subsection applies, he shall be guilty of an offence and liable on summary conviction to a fine not exceeding level 5 on the standard scale or to imprisonment for a term not exceeding six months or to both.

Subsection (1) applies to any bird of game—

(a)   which has been taken or killed in circumstances which constitute an offence under any of—

   (i)   the Night Poaching Act 1828;
   (ii)   this Act;
   (iii)   the Poaching Prevention Act 1862; or
   (iv)   Part 1 of the Wildlife and Countryside Act 1981 (wildlife); and

(b)   which the person concerned knows or has reason to believe has been so taken or killed.

7   Under existing leases the landlord shall have the game except in certain cases

In all cases where any person shall occupy any land under any lease or agreement made previously to the passing of this Act, except in the cases herein-after next excepted, the lessor or landlord shall have the right of entering upon such land, or of authorizing any other person or persons to enter upon such land, for the purpose of killing or taking the game thereon; and no person occupying any land under any lease or agreement, either for life or for years, made previously to the passing of this Act shall have the right to kill or take the game on such land, except where the right of killing the game upon such land has been expressly granted or allowed to such person by such lease or agreement, or except where upon the original granting or renewal of such lease or agreement a fine or fines shall have been taken, or except where in the case of a term for years such lease or agreement shall have been made for a term exceeding twenty-one years.

8 **This Act not to affect any existing or future agreements respecting game, nor any rights of manor, forest, chase, or warren**

Provided always, that nothing in this Act contained shall authorize any person seised or possessed of or holding any land to kill or take the game, or to permit any other person to kill or take the game upon such land, in any case where, by any deed, grant, lease, or any written or parol demise or contract, a right of entry upon such land for the purpose of killing or taking the game hath been or hereafter shall be reserved or retained by or given or allowed to any grantor, lessor, landlord, or other person whatsoever; nor shall anything in this Act contained defeat or diminish any reservation, exception, covenant, or agreement already contained in any private Act of Parliament, deed, or other writing, relating to the game upon any land, nor in any manner prejudice the rights ..., or of any lord of any manor, lordship, or royalty, or reputed manor, lordship, or royalty, or of any steward of the crown of any manor, lordship, or royalty appertaining to his Majesty.

9 **This Act not to affect any of His Majesty's Forest Rights, &c**

Provided also, that nothing in this Act contained shall in any way alter or affect the prerogative, rights, or privileges of his Majesty, ...

10 **Not to affect any Cattlegates or Right of Common. Lord of manor to have the game on the wastes**

Provided also, that nothing herein contained shall be deemed to give to any owner of cattlegates or rights of common upon or over any wastes or commons any interest or privilege which such owner was not possessed of before the passing of this Act, nor to authorize such owner of cattlegates or rights of common to pursue or kill the game found on such wastes or commons; and that nothing herein contained shall defeat or diminish the rights or privileges which any lord of any manor, lordship, or royalty, or reputed manor, lordship, or royalty, or any steward of the crown of any manor, lordship, or royalty appertaining to his Majesty, may, before the passing of this Act, have exercised in or over such wastes or commons; and that the lord or steward of the crown of every manor, lordship, or royalty, or reputed manor, lordship, or royalty, shall have the right to pursue and kill the game upon the wastes or commons within such manor, lordship, or royalty, or reputed manor, lordship, or royalty, and to authorize any other person or persons to enter upon such wastes or commons for the purpose of pursuing and killing the game thereon.

11 Landlord, having the Game, may authorize others to kill it

Where the lessor or landlord shall have reserved to himself the right of killing the game upon any land, it shall be lawful for him to authorize any other person or persons to enter upon such land for the purpose of pursuing and killing game thereon.

12 Where the landlord, &c. has the right to the game, in exclusion of the occupier, the occupier shall be liable to a penalty for killing it

Where the right of killing the game upon any land is by this Act given to any lessor or landlord, in exclusion of the right of the occupier of such land, or where such exclusive right hath been or shall be specially reserved by or granted to, or doth or shall belong to, the lessor, landlord, or any person whatsoever other than the occupier of such land, then and in every such case, if the occupier of such land shall pursue, kill, or take any game upon such land, or shall give permission to any other person so to do, without the authority of the lessor, landlord, or other person having the right of killing the game upon such land, such occupier shall, on conviction thereof before two justices of the peace, forfeit and pay for such pursuit such sum of money not exceeding level 1 on the standard scale, and for every head of game so killed or taken such sum of money not exceeding level 1 on the standard scale, as to the convicting justices shall seem meet, ...

13 Lords of manors may appoint gamekeepers. Powers of gamekeepers of manors

It shall be lawful for any lord of a manor, lordship, or royalty, or reputed manor, lordship, or royalty, or any steward of the crown of any manor, lordship, or royalty appertaining to his Majesty, by writing under hand and seal, or in case of a body corporate, then under the seal of such body corporate, to appoint one or more person or persons as a gamekeeper or gamekeepers to preserve or kill the game within the limits of such manor, lordship, or royalty, or reputed manor, lordship, or royalty, for the use of such lord or steward thereof, ...

14 Lords of Manors may grant Deputations

It shall be lawful for any lord of a manor, lordship, or royalty, or reputed manor, lordship, or royalty, or any steward of the crown of any manor, lordship, or royalty appertaining to his Majesty, to appoint and depute any person whatever, whether acting as a gamekeeper to any other person or not, or whether retained and paid for as the male servant of any other person or not, to be a gamekeeper for any such manor, lordship, or royalty, or reputed manor, lordship, or royalty, or for such division or district of such manor, lordship, or royalty as such lord or steward of the crown shall think fit, and to authorize such person, as gamekeeper, to kill game within the same for his own use or for the use of any other person or persons who may be specified in such appointment or deputation, and also to give to such person all such powers and authorities as may by virtue of this Act be given to any gamekeeper of a manor; and no person so appointed gamekeeper, and empowered to kill game for his own use or for the use of any other person so specified as aforesaid, and not killing any game for the use of the lord or steward of the crown of the manor, lordship, or royalty, or reputed manor, lordship, or royalty, for which such deputation or appointment shall be given, shall be deemed to be or shall be entered or paid for as the gamekeeper or male servant of the lord or steward making such appointment or deputation, anything in any Act or Acts contained to the contrary notwithstanding.

15 Regulations respecting appointment of gamekeepers in Wales

It shall be lawful for every person who shall be entitled to kill the game upon any lands in Wales of the clear annual value of five hundred pounds, whereof he shall be seised in fee or as of freehold, or to which he shall otherwise be beneficially entitled in his own right, if such lands shall not be within the bounds of any manor, lordship, or royalty, or if, being within the same, they shall have been enfranchised or alienated therefrom, to appoint, by writing under his hand and seal, a gamekeeper or gamekeepers to preserve or kill the game over and upon such his lands, and also over and upon the lands in Wales of any other person, who, being entitled to kill the game upon such last-mentioned lands, shall by licence in writing authorize him to appoint a gamekeeper or gamekeepers to preserve or kill the game thereupon, such last-mentioned lands not being within the bounds of any manor, lordship, or royalty, or having been enfranchised or alienated therefrom; ...

16 All appointments of gamekeepers to be registered with the clerk of the peace

Provided always, that no appointment or deputation of any person as a gamekeeper by virtue of this Act shall be valid unless and until it shall be registered with the clerk of the peace for the county, riding, division, liberty, franchise, city, or town wherein the manor, lordship, or royalty, or reputed manor, lordship, or royalty, or the lands, shall be situate, for or in respect of which such person shall have been appointed gamekeeper; and in case the appointment of any person as gamekeeper shall expire or be revoked, by dismissal or otherwise, all powers and authorities given to him by virtue of this Act shall immediately cease and determine.

24 Penalty for destroying or taking the Eggs of Game, &c

If any person not having the right of killing the game upon any land, nor having permission from the person having such right, shall wilfully take out of the nest or destroy in the nest upon such land the eggs of any bird of game, or of any swan, wild duck, teal, or widgeon, or shall knowingly have in his house, shop, possession, or control any such eggs so taken, every such person shall, on conviction thereof before two justices of the peace, forfeit and pay for every egg so taken or destroyed, or so found in his house, shop, possession, or control, such sum of money, not exceeding level 1 on the standard scale, as to the said justices shall seem meet, ...

30 Penalty on persons trespassing in the day-time upon lands in search of game. Where the Occupier of the Land, not being entitled to the Game, allows any Person to kill it, the Party entitled to the Game may enforce the Penalty

... if any person whatsoever shall commit any trespass by entering or being in the daytime upon any land in search or pursuit of game, or woodcocks, snipes, ... or conies, such person shall, on conviction thereof before a justice of the peace, forfeit and pay such sum of money, not exceeding level 3 on the standard scale, as to the justice shall seem meet, ...; and if any persons to the number of five or more together shall commit any trespass, by entering or being in the daytime upon any land in search or pursuit of game, or woodcocks, snipes, ... or conies, each of such persons shall, on conviction thereof before a justice of the peace, forfeit and pay such sum of money, not exceeding level 4 on the standard scale as to the said justice shall seem meet, ...: Provided always, that any person charged with any such trespass shall be at liberty to prove, by way of defence, any matter which would have been a defence to an action at law for such trespass; save and except that the leave and licence of the occupier of the land so trespassed upon shall not be a sufficient defence in any case where the landlord, lessor, or other person shall have the right of killing the game upon such land by virtue of any reservation or otherwise, as herein-before mentioned; but such landlord, lessor, or other person shall, for the purpose of prosecuting for each of the two offences herein last before mentioned, be deemed to be the legal occupier of such land, whenever the actual occupier thereof shall have given such leave or licence; and that the lord or steward of the crown of any manor, lordship, or royalty, or reputed manor, lordship, or royalty, shall be deemed to be the legal occupier of the land of the wastes or commons within such manor, lordship, or royalty, or reputed manor, lordship, or royalty.

31   Trespassers in search of game may be required to quit the land, and to tell their names and abodes, and in case of refusal may be arrested. Penalty. Persons arrested must be discharged unless brought before a justice within 12 hours

Where any person shall be found on any land ... in the day-time, in search or pursuit of game, or woodcocks, snipes, ... or conies, it shall be lawful for any person having the right of killing the game upon such land, by virtue of any reservation or otherwise, as herein-before mentioned, or for the occupier of the land (whether there shall or shall not be any such right by reservation or otherwise), or for any gamekeeper or servant of either of them, or for any person authorized by either of them, ..., to require the person so found forthwith to quit the land whereon he shall be so found, and also to tell his christian name, surname, and place of abode; and in case such person shall, after being so required, offend by refusing to tell his real name or place of abode, or by giving such a general description of his place of abode as shall be illusory for the purpose of discovery, or by wilfully continuing or returning upon the land, it shall be lawful for the party so requiring as aforesaid, and also for any person acting by his order and in his aid, to apprehend such offender, and to convey him or cause him to be conveyed as soon as conveniently may be before a justice of the peace; and such offender (whether so apprehended or not), upon being convicted of any such offence before a justice of the peace, shall forfeit and pay such sum of money, not exceeding level 1 on the standard scale, as to the convicting justice shall seem meet, ...: Provided always, that no person so apprehended shall, on any pretence whatsoever, be detained for a longer period than twelve hours from the time of his apprehension until he shall be brought before some justice of the peace; and that if he cannot, on account of the absence or distance of the residence of any such justice of the peace, or owing to any other reasonable cause, be brought before a justice of the peace within such twelve hours as aforesaid, then the person so apprehended shall be discharged, but may nevertheless be proceeded against for his offence by summons or warrant, according to the provisions herein-after mentioned, as if no such apprehension had taken place.

31A Powers of constables in relation to trespassers

The powers conferred by section 31 above to require a person found on land as mentioned in that section to quit the land and to tell his christian name, surname, and place of abode shall also be exercisable by a police constable.

32 Penalty on Persons found armed using Violence, &c

Where any persons, to the number of five or more together, shall be found on any land, ..., in the daytime, in search or pursuit of game, or woodcocks, snipes, ... or conies, any of such persons being then and there armed with a gun, and such persons or any of them shall then and there, by violence, intimidation, or menace, prevent or endeavour to prevent any persons authorized as herein-before mentioned from approaching such persons so found, or any of them, for the purpose of requiring them or any or them to quit the land whereon they shall be so found, or to tell their or his own christian name, surname, or place of abode respectively, as herein-before mentioned, every person so offending by such violence, intimidation, or menace as aforesaid, and every person then and there aiding or abetting such offender, shall, upon being convicted thereof before two justices of the peace, forfeit and pay for every such offence such penalty, not exceeding level 5 on the standard scale, as to the convicting justices shall seem meet ...; which said penalty shall be in addition to and independent of any other penalty to which any such person may be liable for any other offence against this Act.

34 What to be deemed daytime

For the purposes of this Act the daytime shall be deemed to commence at the beginning of the last hour before sunrise, and to conclude at the expiration of the first hour after sunset.

35 The Provisions as to trespassers not to apply to persons hunting, &c

Provided always, that the aforesaid provisions against trespassers and persons found on any land shall not extend to any lord or any steward of the crown of any manor, lordship, or royalty, or reputed manor, lordship, or royalty, nor to any gamekeeper lawfully appointed by such lord or steward within the limits of such manor, lordship, or royalty, or reputed manor, lordship, or royalty.

36   Game may be taken from Trespassers not delivering up the same when demanded

When any person shall be found by day or night upon any land, ..., in search or pursuit of game, and shall then and there have in his possession any game which shall appear to have been recently killed, it shall be lawful for any person having the right of killing the game upon such land, by virtue of any reservation or otherwise, as herein-before mentioned, or for the occupier of such land (whether there shall or shall not be any such right by reservation or otherwise), or for any gamekeeper or servant or either of them, or ... for any person acting by the order and in aid of any of the said several persons, to demand from the person so found such game in his possession, and, in case such person shall not immediately deliver up such game, to seize and take the same from him, for the use of the person entitled to the game upon such land, ...

41   Time for Proceedings, and Mode of enforcing the Appearance of Offenders

The prosecution for every offence punishable upon summary conviction by virtue of this Act shall be commenced within three calendar months after the commission of the offence, ...

46   This Act not to preclude actions for trespass, but no double proceedings for the same trespass

Provided always, that nothing in this Act contained shall prevent any person from proceeding by way of civil action to recover damages in respect of any trespass upon his land, whether committed in pursuit of game or otherwise, save and except that where any proceedings shall have been instituted under the provisions of this Act against any person for or in respect of any trespass, no action at law shall be maintainable for the same trespass by any person at whose instance or with whose concurrence or assent such proceedings shall have been instituted, but that such proceedings shall in such case be a bar to any such action, ...

48   Act not to extend to Scotland or Ireland

Nothing in this Act contained shall extend to Scotland or Ireland.

B3   Wildlife and Countryside Act 1981

Schedule 2
Birds Which May be Killed or Taken

Part I
Outside the Close Season

Common name	Scientific name
Capercaillie	Tetrao urogallus
Coot	Fulica atra
Duck, Tufted	Aythya fuligula
Gadwall	Anas strepera
Goldeneye	Bucephala clangula
Goose, Canada	Branta canadensis
Goose, Greylag	Anser anser
Goose, Pink-footed	Anser brachyrhynchus
Goose, White-fronted (in England and Wales only)	Anser albifrons
Mallard	Anas platyrhynchos
Moorhen	Gallinula chloropus
Pintail	Anas acuta
Plover, Golden	Pluvialis apricaria
Pochard	Aythya ferina
Shoveler	Anas clypeata
Snipe, Common	Gallinago gallinago
Teal	Anas crecca
Wigeon	Anas penelope
Woodcock	Scolopax rusticola

Note. The common name or names given in the first column of this Schedule are included by way of guidance only; in the event of any dispute or proceedings, the common name or names shall not be taken into account.

B4   Deer Act 1991

Schedule 1
Close Seasons

CHINESE WATER DEER (*Hydropotes inermis*)	
Buck	1st April to 31st October inclusive
Doe	1st April to 31st October inclusive
FALLOW DEER (*Dama dama*)	
Buck	1st May to 31st July inclusive
Doe	1st April to 31st October inclusive
RED DEER (*Cervus Elaphus*)	
Dtags	1st May to 31st July inclusive
Hinds	1st April to 31st October inclusive
RED/SIKA DEER HYBRIDS	
Stags	1st May to 31st July inclusive
Hinds	1st April to 31st October inclusive
ROE DEER (*Capreolus capreolus*)	
Buck	1st November to 31st March inclusive
Doe	1st April to 31st October inclusive
SIKA DEER (*Cervus Nippon*)	
Stags	1st May to 31st July inclusive
Hinds	1st April to 31st October inclusive

B5   Deer Act 1991

Schedule 2
Prohibited Firearms and Ammunition

1   Any smooth-bore gun.

2   Any rifle having a calibre of less than .240 inches or a muzzle of energy of less than 2305 joules (1700 foot pounds).

3   Any air gun, air rifle or air pistol.

4   Any cartridge for use in a smooth-bore gun.

5   Any bullet for use in a rifle other than a soft-nosed or hollow-nosed bullet.

Index